The Birds of Paradise

The Birds of Paradise

MICHAEL EVERETT

Illustrated with plates by John Gould, W. Hart and J. G. Keulemans and original paintings by Peter Hayman.

G. P. PUTNAM'S SONS, NEW YORK

Contents

Family PTILONORHYNCHIDAE: Bowerbirds

A QUARTO BOOK

Published by
G. P. Putnam's Sons
200 Madison Avenue
New York, N.Y. 10016

© Copyright 1978 Quarto Limited
All rights reserved
No part of this publication may be reproduced in any
form or by any means without permission in writing
from the publisher. Published simultaneously in
Canada by Longman Canada Limited, Toronto.

Library of Congress Catalog Card Number: 78-60216
ISBN: 399-12251-6

This book was designed and produced by
Quarto Publishing Limited
13 New Burlington Street, London W1

Art Director: Robert Morley
Editor: Nicholas Fry
Editorial Assistant: Corinne Molesworth
Picture Research: Anne-Marie Ehrlich

Colour plates originated by Starf Photolito SRL,
Rome, Italy and Welbeck Litho Plates Ltd., Bromley,
Kent, England.
Phototypeset by Vantage Photosetting Ltd.,
Southampton, England

Printed in Hong Kong by Leefung-Asco Printers Ltd.

JOHN GOULD *(1804–81)*,
famous English ornithologist and illustrator.

Introduction

IT IS OFTEN SAID THAT BEAUTY is in the eye of the beholder. By this token, the most unlikely and unprepossessing of birds appeal to many ornithologists who may be attracted by their shape, movement, behaviour and voice rather than by simple beauty of plumage. Ornithologists will seldom abandon their own 'special' birds and agree with one another that any one bird group is undeniably beautiful – but this is surely the case when birds of paradise are considered. Only an ornithological philistine would deny them one of the very top places in a list of the world's most beautiful birds. Their plumage is often exotic, both in the vividness of its colouring and in the fantastic adornment it includes – adornments which are among the most bizarre of the bird world. As if this were not enough, the most picturesque species also have some of the most extraordinarily beautiful displays known among birds. It is small wonder, then, that birds of paradise have a fascination which is all their own.

Their generally drabber and much less spectacular relatives the bowerbirds are no less interesting, although in a rather different way. Instead of exotic plumage, they have a unique display system in which they use a variety of elaborately constructed bowers to attract and win their mates. These bowers are often beautifully decorated with all manner of objects and, incredibly, are even painted by some species.

Unfortunately, only a very small number of ornithologists have been lucky enough to study these fabulous birds in the wild. Many species are not at all well known and for some even the most basic details of their daily lives remain a mystery. Some have been studied in captivity; one has never been seen alive by ornithologists; and there remains the intriguing possibility that one or two species have still to be discovered. Even so, much has been written about them and, not surprisingly, they have attracted the attention of a number of great bird artists. In this book, many of the illustrations are reproductions of the superb portraits by John Gould, W. Hart and J. G. Keulemans, from R. Bowdler Sharpe's classic *Monograph of the Paradiseidae, or Birds of Paradise, and Ptilonorhynchidae, or Bower Birds* (1891–98). The remaining artwork, including plates of those species not known to or not featured by the 19th-century painters, is by Peter Hayman, one of the foremost bird artists of our own time.

The text here is a brief summary of the work of many authors, including a number of present-day observers, but owes most to the classic work of the late E. Thomas Gilliard, whose *Birds of Paradise and Bower Birds* has been the standard work since its publication in 1969. Much more recently, another splendid book has appeared, *The Birds of Paradise and Bower Birds*, by William T. Cooper and Joseph M. Forshaw, which brings in much of the latest information gathered since Gilliard's day and, in particular, presents a magnificent series of entirely new colour plates by Cooper. This too, along with the papers written since Gilliard, has been widely consulted. A full list of all the authorities for the various facts and opinions recorded in this book would inevitably be a very long one, so for the most part the sources consulted are not mentioned individually: all may be found by reference to the very comprehensive bibliographies included in the two major works mentioned above. A selected bibliography on page 144 lists the main references but concentrates on those most likely to be available to the general reader.

This book makes no pretence to completeness and is only intended as a well-illustrated introduction to two fascinating groups of birds; in a sense it has been written as a more 'popular' companion to the much more detailed works of Gilliard and Cooper and Forshaw. If it promotes further interest in these birds by introducing them to a wider public, and if it helps to promote some further study and conservation, then it will have served its purpose.

MICHAEL EVERETT

The two families

BIRDS OF PARADISE AND BOWERBIRDS belong to two closely-related families within the Order Passeriformes, the major bird grouping which brings together what are commonly called the 'perching birds'. A brief mention of some of the main points surrounding their evolution and inter-relationships is made later. Within the two families, birds are grouped together into genera (sing. genus), each genus containing one or more species. Under the universally adopted Linnaean system of nomenclature, every species has its own unique scientific name, comprising two words, in Latin but commonly employing Latinized forms of words from other languages, especially Ancient Greek. The first of these two words (which may be shared by two or more birds) indicates the genus and the second, which is adjectival, the species within the genus – the two together forming the species name. How this works can be seen by consulting the species list on page 9.

A third Latin word may be added to the species name to identify the subspecies or geographical race of a species: populations from different parts of a bird's range, which may be isolated from one another or may intergrade, are often distinguishable by differences in size or coloration sufficient to merit recognition as subspecies – although this is one area of bird systematics where differences of opinion may be as numerous as subspecies themselves and there is frequent disagreement among authorities for this or that name. Subspeciation is well marked in many birds of paradise and bowerbirds, described here at species level.

The use of a standardized system of scientific names overcomes the confusion which can arise with vernacular names – which may be the same for two totally different species. Equally, several different vernacular names may be in current use for one species. The birds of paradise and bowerbirds are a case in point: during the last hundred years or so their scientific names have chopped and changed a great deal as more has come to light concerning their possible lines of evolution and their inter-relationships; but they are now more or less standardized and generally agreed, with a few minor exceptions. Their English names, however, still present difficulties as virtually no two books use the same names

Jerome Bonaparte, (1822–91), son of the King of Westphalia. An ornithologist who attained notoriety by defying convention, naming and describing a bird discovered by somebody else.

for some species. Reference to Gilliard's book and the more or less contemporary *Birds of New Guinea*, of which he was co-author, illustrates the point well enough. In this book, the scientific and English names are those used by Gilliard, subject to a few important amendments recommended by Dr R. Schodde in his 1975 Provisional Checklist, compiled for the Royal Australasian Ornithologists' Union – one of which, incidentally, is the one-word spelling of 'bowerbird'. In a few cases, alternative English names are given.

A number of species, especially among the birds of paradise, have names every bit as exotic as the birds themselves. Some are named after their discoverers, or those who first described them for science, or in honour of a colleague or patron. Some names reflect the custom of naming birds after contemporary European royalty. In this connection it is amusing to recall one political side-swipe perpetuated in a scientific name. Prince Bonaparte, an ornithologist of some renown and a nephew of Napoleon, introduced *respublica* for Wilson's Bird of Paradise – reflecting his republican ideals. Unfortunately he is probably better remembered among ornithologists for having cheated in that he described and named this bird when it had in fact been discovered by others, against all the ethics of the process of nomenclature . . . but that is another story!

SPECIES LIST

Family PARADISAEIDAE: Birds of Paradise

Loria loriae	Loria's Bird of Paradise	*Astrapia nigra*	Arfak Astrapia Bird of Paradise
Loboparadisea sericea	Wattle-billed Bird of Paradise	*Astrapia splendidissima*	Splendid Astrapia Bird of Paradise
Cnemophilus macgregorii	Sickle-crested Bird of Paradise	*Astrapia mayeri*	Ribbon-tailed Bird of Paradise
Macgregoria pulchra	Macgregor's Bird of Paradise	*Astrapia stephaniae*	Princess Stephanie Bird of Paradise
Lycocorax pyrrhopterus	Paradise *or* Silky Crow	*Astrapia rothschildi*	Huon Astrapia Bird of Paradise
Manucodia ater	Glossy-mantled Manucode	*Lophorina superba*	Superb Bird of Paradise
Manucodia jobiensis	Jobi Manucode	*Parotia wahnesi*	Wahnes' Six-wired Bird of Paradise
Manucodia chalybatus	Crinkle-collared Manucode	*Parotia sefilata*	Arfak Six-wired Bird of Paradise
Manucodia comrii	Curl-crested Manucode	*Parotia carolae*	Queen Carola's Six-wired Bird of Paradise
Manucodia keraudrenii	Trumpet Bird *or* Trumpet Manucode	*Parotia lawesi*	Lawe's Six-wired Bird of Paradise
Ptiloris paradiseus	Paradise Riflebird	*Pteridophora alberti*	King of Saxony Bird of Paradise
Ptiloris victoriae	Queen Victoria *or* Victoria Riflebird	*Cicinnurus regius*	King Bird of Paradise
Ptiloris magnificus	Magnificent Riflebird	*Diphyllodes magnificus*	Magnificent Bird of Paradise
Semioptera wallacei	Wallace's Standard Wing	*Diphyllodes respublica*	Wilson's Bird of Paradise
Seleucidis melanoleuca	Twelve-wired Bird of Paradise	*Paradisaea apoda*	Greater Bird of Paradise
Paradigalla carunculata	Long-tailed Paradigalla	*Paradisaea raggiana*	Count Raggi's Bird of Paradise
Paradigalla brevicauda	Short-tailed Paradigalla	*Paradisaea minor*	Lesser Bird of Paradise
Drepanornis albertisii	Black-billed Sickle-billed Bird of Paradise	*Paradisaea decora*	Goldie's Bird of Paradise
Drepanornis bruijnii	White-billed Sickle-billed Bird of Paradise	*Paradisaea rubra*	Red Bird of Paradise
Epimachus fastosus	Black Sickle-billed Bird of Paradise	*Paradisaea guilielmi*	Emperor of Germany Bird of Paradise
Epimachus meyeri	Brown Sickle-billed Bird of Paradise	*Paradisaea rudolphi*	Blue Bird of Paradise

Family PTILONORHYNCHIDAE: Bowerbirds

Ailuroedus buccoides	White-eared Catbird	*Prionodura newtoniana*	Golden Bowerbird
Ailuroedus crassirostris	Green Catbird	*Sericulus aureus*	Golden Regent Bowerbird
Ailuroedus melanotis	Spotted *or* Black-eared Catbird	*Sericulus bakeri*	Adelbert Regent Bowerbird
Ailuroedus dentirostris	Tooth-billed Catbird *or* Tooth-billed or Stagemaker Bowerbird	*Sericulus chrysocephalus*	Australian Regent Bowerbird *or* Australian Regentbird
Archboldia papuensis	Archbold's Bowerbird	*Ptilonorhynchus violaceus*	Satin Bowerbird
Amblyornis inornatus	Vogelkop Gardener Bowerbird	*Chlamydera nuchalis*	Great *or* Great Grey Bowerbird
Amblyornis macgregoriae	Macgregor's Gardener Bowerbird	*Chlamydera lauterbachi*	Lauterbach's Bowerbird
Amblyornis subalaris	Striped Gardener Bowerbird	*Chlamydera maculata*	Spotted Bowerbird
Amblyornis flavifrons	Yellow-fronted Gardener Bowerbird	*Chlamydera cerviniventris*	Fawn-breasted Bowerbird

Discovery and exploitation

BEFORE LOOKING AT THESE BIRDS in more detail, it is necessary to examine civilized man's first encounters with them, the history of his exploitation of some of the more exotically-plumed species and the work of a relatively small group of naturalists who are responsible for most of our present knowledge of birds of paradise and bowerbirds.

It was not until 1511 that the first Europeans, Portuguese adventurers from Goa, set eyes on New Guinea. In the years that followed, the first landings were made and it is certain that these early Portuguese explorations confirmed the origins of some of the fabulous feathers they must already have seen or known about. It was not long before the Spaniards learned of this new country and in 1545 Ortiz de Retes planted the Spanish flag east of Geelvink Bay and named the new territory 'Nueva Guinea', having been reminded by the natives he encountered there of those he had known in African Guinea. The Spanish presence was to last little more than a century: they ran into hard times and by 1660 had been replaced by the Dutch, whose East Indies Company gradually took over and established a rule which was to endure (in name at least) for three hundred years.

By the middle of the 18th century the Dutch too were in difficulties and at war with the native Papuans. The first British presence came in 1793, on the Vogelkop, but they too were soon driven out and a second attempt to gain a foothold in 1828 was equally abortive. For most of the 19th century New Guinea and its native inhabit-ants resisted all European intrusions, small as they were, and it was not until 1883 that European influence became a really serious factor. The Australians established Port Moresby in that year, and laid claim to Papua; in 1884 the Germans annexed the greater part of the northern half of eastern New Guinea. In 1895, the Dutch and the Australians divided New Guinea between them, drawing a north-south boundary along the 141st meridian – the area to the west becoming Netherlands New Guinea and that in the east what we now know as Papua New Guinea. Dutch sovereignty came to an end in 1962 and the former Netherlands New Guinea duly became Irian Barat and part of Indonesia. Papua New Guinea, long administered from Australia, gained independence in 1974.

Space does not permit us to wander far into the fascinating history of New Guinea, but in terms of ornithological exploration it is important to realize that for most of the three or four centuries of European 'occupation' of the island the white man's involvement was confined to the coastal lowlands. True, there was some penetration of the interior and some notable explorations were carried out, but it was not until fifty years ago that any really large moves were made on the part of settlers, explorers and adventurers, and most of the roads, towns and plantations in eastern New Guinea only date from the era following the second World War. Throughout the pages of the island's history there is the theme of conflict with the native inhabitants, the Papuans, most of

This stretch of lowland jungle along the Purari River in New Guinea is typical of the kind of terrain where birds of paradise are found.

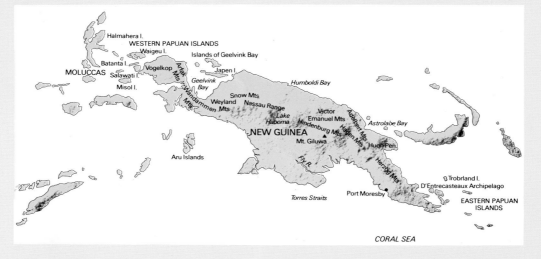

CORAL SEA

whom were of Australian or Melanesian origins. Many of them still lived in a culture akin to that of the Stone Age, and in some areas they achieved an almost legendary status through their habits of head-hunting and cannibalism. Bearing in mind the inhospitable nature of parts of the interior, and the dangers inherent in going there, it is hardly surprising that so much of New Guinea long remained unknown.

What, then, is the nature of this great island where most of the birds of paradise and many of the bowerbirds are found? It lies just south of the Equator and off the north and north-eastern extremities of Australia, covering an area of some 808,000 square kilometres *(312,000 square miles)*; it is nearly 2400 kilometres *(1500 miles)* in length and a little over 640 kilometres *(400 miles)* across at its broadest point. Geologically and biologically, it is closely associated with Australia and is separated from it by relatively shallow seas – the two are believed to have been joined at one time; together, Australia and New Guinea form the Australo-Papuan region, a huge sub-continent bounded on three sides by deep seas and isolated from South-east Asia for around 60 million years.

Basically, New Guinea is divided longitudinally by a chain of massive, jagged mountains, with peaks rising to 5000 metres *(16,500 feet)* in the west and topping 4600 metres *(15,000 feet)* in many other places. Passes are few and the only major break in this huge mountain barrier is at the isthmus south of Geelvink Bay – thus, an effective wall has been thrown up separating the wildlife in the tropical and sub-tropical zones on either side of the mountains. In many places there are high mountain valleys within the main massif, some of them very fertile. The whole mountain system – and indeed the whole of New Guinea – is recent and unstable, and is thus subject to frequent earth tremors.

At its sides, the mountain range drops in steep eroded slopes and sheer faces into the rain forest which covers much of the plains country below. The uplands are drained via many large rivers to the north and south which wind through the lower-lying jungles and mangrove swamps, sometimes for hundreds of miles, on their way to the sea. Many of these rivers have wide mouths, behind which there are often vast areas of cane grass with pockets of swamp-forest. Further inland lies the dense tropical rain-forest belt. A few species of birds of paradise and bowerbirds have spread down into this lower-lying zone, but by far the majority are found in the life-zone above, the mid-mountain forest which begins to replace the tropical lower forest from about 1400 metres *(4500 feet)*. Here, the mountain forest is largely of oak, but in due course this is replaced (at around 2300 metres / *7500 feet)* by beech. Beyond 3000 metres *(10,000 feet)*, pine forest takes over, extending up to the limit of tree growth which in New Guinea lies somewhere between 3400 and 3700 metres *(11,000 and 12,000 feet)*.

One more important geological feature remains to be mentioned, one which in its own way forms a barrier between different animal communities which is every bit as effective as the main mountain chain itself. This is the Central Depression which is drained by all the main rivers of northern New Guinea and runs for about 1600 kilometres *(1000 miles)* eastwards from the northern edge of the Snow Mountains. Birds of paradise provide just one example of how closely related types can be isolated from one another by such a barrier: two pairs of species of Six-wired Birds of Paradise and two from the genus *Paradisaea* are present on either side, destined never to meet and separated as effectively as if they were on islands in the sea.

In terms of weather, there are two main seasons in New Guinea, the 'dry', from May to around November, and then the 'wet', which lasts through until April. Annual rainfall may be as high as 760 centimetres *(300 inches)* in some areas and it is worth mentioning that by the standards people are used to in many other parts of the world even the dry season is relatively wet. The seasons and their rainfall influence the availability of food as far as birds are concerned and, like most New Guinea birds, birds of paradise reach the peak of their courtship and display towards the end of the dry season and breed as the wet season begins.

To the ornithologist, New Guinea – and indeed the whole Australo-Papuan region – supports a wealth of bird families and species; perhaps the most interesting are those which occur here and nowhere else, of which Australo-Papua can boast more than any other region in the world except the tropical New World. Among these are the cassowaries, the emus, the megapodes, the lyrebirds, the flowerpeckers and the honeyeaters – and, of course, the birds of paradise and the bowerbirds.

It seems likely that bird of paradise plumes were known outside New Guinea at least 2000 years ago, appearing in Western Asia and perhaps even Eastern Europe via the ancient trade routes from the Far East. But for many centuries real familiarity with these plumes was confined to the native peoples of New Guinea; the exotic ornamental feathers of some species, usually from fully mature males, but also to some extent certain feathers from less spectacular species, have long been prized by the Papuans, especially for use in decorative head-dresses. This use of plumes continues down to the present day, and although it may have declined or even ceased in some areas it has actually grown in popularity in others in. modern times: with the coming of peace to many highland areas, a greater mobility among the native people and a higher standard of affluence, trading in plumes has increased and there is a real demand for larger quantities of some of them. It seems probable that an increasing population has led to greater pressures too and there can be no doubt that the availability of firearms has made plume-hunting easier. The traditional method of shooting birds of paradise with three- or four-pronged arrows, from cunningly concealed hides or blinds beside males' traditional display perches, is still used but may now be on the decline.

In passing, it is worth mentioning one intriguing aspect of these traditional methods which Gilliard described in his monograph from the Wahgi Valley region. Here he found that in the case of Count Raggi's Bird of Paradise (always a firm favourite of plume-hunters) the display trees used by individual males were actually 'owned' by individual hunters, who seemed to respect one another's ownership of tree and bird. Each male would be watched and guarded by its 'owner' until it was considered that its plumage had reached the climax of its development – and then, and only then, it would be shot.

A detailed study of the use of plumes for human ornamentation, covering both native customs and the pressures brought to bear on individual species, would be of enormous value, both in gaining a better knowledge of the birds' relevance to the Papuan way of life and in learning more about the conservation requirements of the species most involved. It is pleasing to know that the Wildlife Service of the Papua New Guinea government aims to cover these very issues in a new and exciting research programme, as well as doing much more work on the basic distribution and ecology of the birds. One offshoot of this research will be the establishment of reasonable harvesting levels, which will allow the traditional hunting for plumes to continue without causing any one species to decline in numbers or become a rarity through over-exploitation. The realization that bird of paradise conservation is as closely tied to sociological considerations as to ecological requirements, is of the utmost importance.

Clearly the killing of adult male birds of paradise has been traditional in Papua for centuries. The important question is whether this has affected the birds' numbers in any way and whether it is a practice that should be discontinued, or at least discouraged. Obviously some of the answers will depend on the outcome of the research programme mentioned above, but it is possible to draw some conclusions from what is known already. While it is apparently true that the cropping process may have caused the local rarity of a few species, the overall effect on numbers has not been great and on the face of it there seems no reason why the practice should not be allowed to continue. Whether there is any cause for alarm resulting from the increase in internal trading, and whether there is a case for stricter control as a result of this, remains to be seen. In the meantime, it is probably safe to say that at present no species is in great danger as a result of plume-hunting. Furthermore, it seems that the birds themselves have a natural defence-mechanism of their own which allows them to withstand a certain amount of hunting: with their arena–display type of behaviour, their habit of living apart from the females for most of their lives and their polygyny they seem to be able to maintain reasonable numbers; even if they suffer temporary large losses, their species are seldom in danger because normally only fully-plumed males are killed – males in less than perfect plumage are often left alone and both they and birds in only half-developed plumage are fully capable of breeding.

The next question to be asked is whether the great era of plume-collecting by the

R.-P. LESSON *(1794-1849)*,
the first naturalist to see live birds of paradise.

Europeans, which achieved truly massive proportions for some years, had any major consequences. It was not until somewhere around the beginning of the 17th century that bird of paradise skins arrived in any numbers in Europe. The incredible beauty

SIR WILLIAM MACGREGOR *(1837-1919)*,
British administrator and naturalist.

of many of them attracted attention in two ways – as highly-valued treasures and as items of great scientific interest. As early as 1605, the first accurate description of two species, the Great and Lesser Birds of Paradise, were made from specimen skins, but while the amount of information on these exciting birds grew slowly and steadily over the next two centuries, with more species being described, no naturalist had ever seen the birds in the wild until the Frenchman Lesson spent a fortnight at Dorey in 1824. He saw two species already known to science, the Lesser and King Birds of Paradise, and described two new ones, the Trumpet Bird and the Glossy-mantled Manucode. After him, in the 1850s, there came the great English naturalist Alfred Wallace, who found the remarkable Standard Wing which bears his name.

Since the days of Lesson and Wallace, a great many naturalists have been to New Guinea, such as Sir William Macgregor who led an expedition to the Vanupa river in 1896 and reported seeing *Macgregoria pulchra*, Macgregor's Bird of Paradise. Nevertheless, it is to the plume-hunters that one must turn for the earliest information, largely through the specimens they obtained since unfortunately very few of them kept detailed written records. Among other things, they sent back apparent rarities, now believed to be hybrids, and of course it was they who produced the only evidence we have of the existence of the Yellow-fronted Gardener Bowerbird – three or four skins, all males, of a species that has still eluded all attempts to find it in the wild.

Hunting and trading in plumes was widespread in the mid-19th century, however it did not achieve significant proportions until 1873–74 when Holland, Germany and Great Britain divided New Guinea into three spheres of influence. Even so, it seems to have been a small-scale affair in the British/Australian sector, although the Blue Bird of Paradise (a particularly difficult species to find and collect) enjoyed a brief vogue during which skins fetched twenty pounds sterling each. Count Raggi's Bird of Paradise was very popular too (fetching one pound per skin) and one friend of Gilliard told him he had obtained six to seven hundred birds in 'good years'. In the German sector, notwithstanding great difficulties (including numerous clashes with cannibals and headhunters) the trade flourished on a much larger scale until the First World War, after which Germany lost all her New Guinea possessions. Tens of thousands of skins, mostly killed by shotguns, were probably obtained in good years and all sold to the government. Of the many species involved, the Blue Bird of Paradise was again the most valuable (reputedly up to forty pounds per skin), followed by the Princess Stephanie and the Count Raggi's. Often, birds of paradise formed the most

ALFRED RUSSEL WALLACE *(1823-1913)*,
author and scientist.

important source of income, especially in the seven years' wait colonists had between planting their copra and its becoming ready for harvesting; copra was the other main money-maker in those times.

In Dutch New Guinea, where most of the European hunting was done in the lowlands of the Vogelkop and along the north coast to Humboldt Bay, bird of paradise skins were for long the main source of income, and official records published in 1910 show that export figures during the previous twenty years regularly numbered between 25,000 and 30,000 birds anually. The Papuans themselves were also much involved in supplying skins for the plumage market. For

Hunters such as these people of Aramia, in the heart of Papua, have traditionally sought bird of paradise plumes to use in decorative head-dresses.

example, many operated through Chinese traders based on Geelvink Bay and there was a flourishing trade in the Aru Islands. In the hinterland of southern New Guinea, above Merauke, the natives had a monopoly; as Gilliard drily remarked 'This was because the Tugeri tribes of that area were fierce hunters of human heads as well as excellent hunters of birds of paradise'.

It has been reliably estimated that something like 80,000 skins per year (and possibly many more) left New Guinea during the heyday of the plumage trade in the years up to the First World War. But the death-knell of the trade was already sounding in Europe, beginning in Britain, where there was a major outcry against the mass slaughter of birds. Egret feathers in particular were popular as articles of fashion, especially in ladies' hats. The general furore in Britain gave rise to an organization which, in our own time, has become one of the world's foremost conservation bodies, the Royal Society for the Protection of Birds. In 1910, the British Parliament passed a bill prohibiting the sale or exchange of bird of paradise plumes and then in 1913, the government of the United States passed important legislation which stopped the importation of bird plumage altogether. It was not long before Canada, Britain, Australia, the Straits Settlements (Malaya), Holland and France followed suit. For birds of paradise, the real answer was to stop the plumage trade at source and here the main target of world opinion was Holland and Dutch New Guinea. Finally, Holland put an end to the commercial killing of the birds: the plumage trade was dead and virtually buried by 1924.

In spite of the colossal numbers of birds killed and exported, there is no evidence that any species suffered any irrecoverable losses during the plumage era, although it seems reasonable to assume that there were some temporary local declines here and there. Poaching and illegal trading appear to have been insignificant during the last half-century. Taking into account the ravages of the plumage trade, plus the traditional collecting of the Papuans, one is forced to conclude that most birds of paradise have come through unscathed. The bowerbirds, with a few exceptions (the Regent Bowerbirds, Macgregor's Gardener Bowerbird and, marginally, the Green Catbird and the Satin Bowerbird) have never been seriously affected by plume-hunting. What is probably an altogether more serious business for many species of both families is the loss or degradation of habitat – always a major problem in bird conservation but nowadays an increasingly acute one in many underdeveloped countries, especially those where large areas of primary forest are present.

As we have mentioned, in New Guinea birds of paradise are predominantly birds of primary forest, more particularly the mid-mountain forest which lies above the tropical rain forest of lower altitudes: no fewer than twenty-six species are confined to the mid-mountain zone, in which some of them have a very limited distribution. Broadly speaking, the vast areas of forest which are so characteristic of New Guinea remained unaltered for centuries except where the Papuans opened up relatively small areas for

Mt. Nautango, part of the precipitous and jungle-covered Crown Prince Range in Bougainville, is the site of a huge copper mining project. Projects such as this destroy the natural habitat of the birds of paradise.

their subsistence agriculture, clearing, planting, cropping and moving on to a new strip of land. Once worked out, the cleared areas, which may have been used continuously for a number of seasons, were abandoned. Secondary vegetation then followed and in its turn was removed as the areas were cultivated once again. The long-term result of all this is poor grassland as fewer and fewer trees survived each successive stage of clearing and cultivation. Gradually, however, the picture changed and whole areas of forest in the mid-mountain beech zone were gone forever; similar effects were caused by the gradual encroachment of European settlers into areas away from the coastal lowlands. One species, the Blue Bird of Paradise, formerly widespread in this habitat zone, has become relatively rare as a direct result of this form of land management and is now common only in inaccessible and remote pockets of surviving forest. A few species have shown some adaptability and are able to exploit the secondary-growth habitats, but often this is only for a limited period of time.

An increase in forestry operations, plus other activities like mining, the establishment of new human settlements, roadbuilding and the opening up of more and more formerly inaccessible areas are all factors of considerable significance in the destruction and alteration of habitat. Agricultural clearances continue, of course, while all these other newer forms of exploitation increase and expand as the inhabitants of the island strive for greater productivity and self-sufficiency – all of which is both under-

standable and correct in a developing situation. But there is growing concern for the natural ecosystems of New Guinea, and particularly for certain special forms of native wildlife (including birds of paradise) as these changes take place – a concern which becomes greater with the realization that the rate of change can only accelerate during the remainder of this century. The modern philosophy of conservation calls for the safeguarding and careful management of natural ecosystems alongside progressive developments aimed at improving the use of natural resources for man's benefit. It says that nature is a resource in itself and is thus important both to man if he wants to live in a balanced environment and in its own right. It also says that progress need not be achieved at the expense of wildlife.

In terms of New Guinea, its forest and its birds of paradise and its bowerbirds, it means that significant areas should be set aside either as natural non-development zones or nature reserves. Fortunately, in Papua New Guinea at least there has been an early recognition of the need for extensive wildlife conservation and one of the most encouraging features of the Wildlife Service programme already mentioned is a priority rating for the establishment and management of adequate reserve areas. The proposed research into the distribution and ecology of birds of paradise included in the programme is just as important: as we shall see, much remains to be found out about these intriguing birds and without a better knowledge of them their future conservation may not succeed.

Origins and evolution

EXPLAINING THE ORIGINS and evolution of any group of birds presents great difficulties, mainly because our knowledge of ancient and ancestral bird forms is so scanty and the fossil evidence, if it exists at all, is often fragmentary. With many groups the best we can do is to study living forms, comparing their physical structure, their general ecology and their patterns of behaviour; from all this we can make a number of deductions and explore a number of theories, finally producing a reasonable analysis of the main trends of their evolution. Not surprisingly, birds of paradise and bowerbirds have stimulated much study and thought among evolutionists. In a general work like this we can only aim to look at the subject in very broad terms, but the interested reader should consult the chapter on evolution in Thomas Gilliard's book and also consider one of the most recent treatises on the subject, 'Evolution in the Birds of Paradise and Bowerbirds, a Resynthesis' by Dr Richard Schodde, published in the Proceedings of the 16th International Ornithological Congress.

It is generally agreed that the Australo-Papuan region was colonized millions of years ago by birds and animals originating in Asia. The resulting avifauna of the region as we see it today includes a number of endemic species, among them the birds of paradise and the bowerbirds. These two families are confined to New Guinea and

THE ALTITUDE RANGE OF THE BIRDS OF PARADISE
The altitudes at which birds of paradise are found range from sea-level (some being confined to islands) to a maximum of nearly 13,000 feet or 3960 metres. Each species occurs within a particular altitudinal range, indicated by the coloured bars, but may be abundant only over a limited band within that range.

Specific altitudes in both metres and feet will be found in the individual entries for each species in the text. The silhouettes shown in the table are not to scale.

PERMANENT SNOW LINE

ICE AT NIGHT ABOVE THIS HEIGHT

SUDDEN CHANGE
FAUNA/FLORA ABOVE THIS HEIGHT

SEA LEVEL

Paradise Riflebird
Victoria Riflebird
Wallace's Standard Wing
White-billed Sickle-billed Bird of Paradise
Red Bird of Paradise
Jobi Manucode
Curl-crested Manucode
King Bird of Paradise
Twelve-wired Bird of Paradise
Glossy-mantled Manucode
Greater Bird of Paradise
Wilson's Bird of paradise
Magnificent Riflebird
Count Raggi's Bird of Paradise
Lesser Bird of Paradise
Goldie's Bird of Paradise
Paradise or Silky Crow
Magnificent Bird of Paradise
Crinkle-collared Manucode
Wahnes' Six-wired Bird of Paradise

some of its satellite islands and to Australia – the Greater Bird of Paradise can be seen on Little Tobago in the Caribbean, but it was introduced there by man in 1909–12. More precisely, birds of paradise and bowerbirds are almost entirely confined to an arc of subtropical and mountain rain forest which runs through New Guinea and down the eastern side of Australia. Of the sixty known species, only eight or nine birds of paradise and one bowerbird have moved into lowland rain forest in New Guinea and only the bowerbirds of the genus *Chlamydera* have left the forest to become birds of grassland, scrub and open woodland in Australia and New Guinea. All authorities agree that the two main groups originated in the mid-mountain forests of New Guinea and spread from there into Australia.

Extensive studies of the physical characteristics of birds of paradise and bowerbirds show them to be closely related. A broad division into three groups is generally recognized: the birds of paradise break down into the cnemophiline group (three species) and the paradisaeine group (thirty-nine

species), while the third group contains the eighteen species of bowerbirds. Various authorities have suggested different classifications, either grouping all sixty species into one family, treating the three groups as separate families, or combining all the birds of paradise into one family and all the bowerbirds into another. The third alternative is the most popular at present and is used in this book. Another important issue concerns the nearest relatives to these birds and here too opinion is divided, some favouring the crows (*Corvidae*) and some the starlings (*Sturnidae*): the latter are current favourites.

Superficially, the birds of paradise appear to be a very diverse group, but in fact they share many common characteristics linking them together and suggesting possible lines of evolutionary development; their most primitive species, those in the cnemophiline group, seem to form a connection between them and the bowerbirds, but it should be emphasized that while it is likely that the cnemophilines shared a common ancestor with bowerbirds, they did not themselves give rise to bowerbirds.

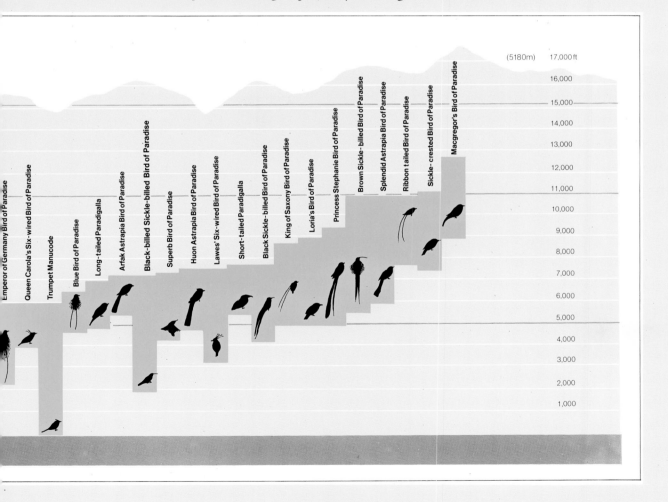

Birds of paradise

THE LAST BIRD OF PARADISE discovered was the Ribbon-tailed, as recently as 1938, and although it is still possible that one or two species have yet to be found in the lesser-known parts of New Guinea it has been assumed by many that the whole family is now known. Today, forty-two species are recognized (a number which might be modified at any time as more is learned about the birds) and of these two are found only in Australia, two are common to Australia and New Guinea, thirty-six are confined to New Guinea and two occur only on the Moluccas.

They range in size from the 150 mm *(6 inch)* King and Wilson's Birds of Paradise to the 710 mm *(28 inch)* Black Sickle-billed Bird of Paradise. While the males are very different in appearance from genus to genus there is a discernible pattern to their ornamentation, with common factors between genera – for example, breast-shields, elongated wire-like central tail-feathers and flank-plumes of various kinds. Females are more obviously similar, often with the same basic pattern of relatively dull plumage and barred underparts in those species where the sexes are different. Highly metallic, iridescent feathers are common to many species. Bill shape is very variable, from short and stout to very long, fine and decurved.

The three cnemophiline species of bird of paradise, Loria's, Wattle-billed and Sickle-crested, are believed to be the most primitive members of the family and to represent the nearest thing to a common ancestor which was presumably a tree-dwelling, monogamous type. All three are believed to be monogamous and to form true pair-bonds and all show sexual differences in plumage. Actually the males show some similarity in the way their display apparatus is positioned around the head – metallic, erectile nasal plumes and yellow gape-wattles in Loria's, greenish-yellow wattles on the bill in Wattle-billed and a small crest in Sickle-crested. Although traditionally placed in three different genera, these species may well be more closely related than this classification suggests.

Macgregor's Bird of Paradise is not unlike the birds of the preceding group in general appearance and like them is a monogamous species; the sexes are alike and both take an active part in rearing the young – not a common feature among birds of paradise whose breeding organization is fully known. Hardly anything is known about the life-history of the Paradise or Silky Crow, which is confined to the Moluccas, but here too the sexes are alike in most details and it is assumed that breeding is of the monogamous kind. This is the most crow-like of all the birds of paradise in appearance and lacks any form of ornamental feathering.

The four species of manucode form an interesting group of rather similar birds, all with basically black plumage with a purple or green gloss and a noticeable 'crinkling' of the feathers. Outwardly they suggest the more primitive species of the cnemophiline group, and like them they are monogamous – but their skulls more closely resemble those of the advanced paradisaeine species.

Of the three species of riflebirds, two are confined to Australia while the third, the Magnificent Riflebird, is found both there and in New Guinea. In contrast to the preceding species, riflebirds are polygynous, with their males displaying in small groups and having iridescent breast-shields and crown-feathers contrasting with otherwise largely dark plumage; all have fairly long, decurved bills. Wallace's Standard Wing is unique among birds of paradise in having two pairs of extremely long white pennants at the bend of the wing, much used in its communal displays when large groups of males gather in traditional display areas. This is another polygynous bird, the males apparently forming clans and living apart from the females for most of the year. A broadly similar breeding organization, in which the male takes no part in the actual nesting operation or the rearing of the young, is thought to be used by the Twelve-wired Bird of Paradise, a particularly striking species in which the male has a great mass of yellow flank-plumes which include six much elongated wire-like projections on either side.

Very little is known about the two Paradigallas. They show some resemblances to the more primitive birds of paradise, but until something is learned of their display system and breeding biology any attempts to relate them to other genera must remain largely conjectural. There are four sickle-billed species, traditionally grouped in two closely-related genera. Hardly anything is known of the breeding biology of the *Drepanornis* species, the Black-billed and White-billed Sickle-bills, but it may well be very similar to the polygynous system employed by the *Epimachus* birds, the Black and Brown Sickle-bills, in which the males maintain special display perches, far apart in traditional trees. All these species, as their names suggest, have long, decurved bills, heavier in *Epimachus*, but they are not specialist insect feeders, as has been suggested, and like most birds of paradise are rather generalized fruit and insect eaters. Additionally, the two *Epimachus* birds differ from the *Drepanornis* species in having very long, graduated tails.

Five species make up the Astrapia group and all are relatively large birds of paradise with very long, graduated tails; they include some of the most beautiful species in the whole family. Four of these birds have very limited distributions in New Guinea and very little is known about any of them; the Ribbon-tailed Bird of Paradise, with its immensely long white central tail-feathers, has the distinction of being the last bird of paradise to be described. The fifth species, the Princess Stephanie Bird of Paradise, is rather better known than its congeners and from its habits we can perhaps deduce a common pattern for the rest of the genus. The Astrapias are all thought to be polygynous, with the males gathering to display in groups in traditional display trees and each individual maintaining his private perch within the arena.

The Superb Bird of Paradise, with its large, erectile blue-green breast-shield and enormous dorsal cape, is a spectacular and fairly well known species. This is another polygynous bird and here the males are believed to display singly and far apart from one another in widely-spaced special display trees. Much the same sort of widely separated traditional display perch system is used by the Six-wired Birds of Paradise of the genus *Parotia* – but here the males actually display on or near the ground and maintain an open area or court which they keep scrupulously clear of vegetation and debris. Their spectacular display-dances include postures in which they expand their elongated flank-plumes outwards and upwards into what has been called the 'umbrella' pose and also swing and rotate their flag-tipped 'wires' which extend from the nape.

The head ornamentation of the male King of Saxony Bird of Paradise is even more fantastic than that of the *Parotia* species – it is perhaps the most bizarre piece of decoration of any kind worn by any bird in the world. From behind the eyes, two incredibly long feather shafts (up to three times the length of the bird's body) sweep backwards, each with a series of blue, enamel-like lobes along their entire length. Not surprisingly, these plumes are much prized for native decoration. This is another species in which the males maintain individual and widely-spaced display places, again in the form of a cleared court on the ground, but this time the court includes a bare vertical sapling which serves as the display perch.

An almost identical system of display, with a cleared court and a vertical display-sapling, is employed by the males of two more polygynous species, Wilson's and the Magnificent Birds of Paradise. Both are incredibly beautiful birds with very vividly-coloured plumage and are unique in having their elongated central tail-feathers curled outwards into an exaggerated lyre shape. Each has an erectile cape on the hindneck and a breast-shield of green feathers which is expanded and pulsated in display. The tiny, brilliant crimson-red King Bird of Paradise is one of the best-known of all the family and is not uncommonly encountered in captivity. The male has extremely long wire-like projections on the central tail-feathers, ending in small whorls of green feathers. In this species, displaying males are again widely spaced and maintain individual display perches, but this time they are typically in a covered situation.

Finally, the genus *Paradisaea*, the largest of the family, includes seven rather similar species which to many people are the epitome of birds of paradise; all are medium-sized birds with elongated, narrowed or wire-like central tail-feathers and most are basically brown or maroon-brown and yellow with large trains of elongated flank-plumes of yellow, orange, red or white. One species, the Blue Bird of Paradise, is much blacker and has bright blue flank-plumes in the mature males – these being the feathers that made this bird one of the most valuable of all during the days of the plumage trade. Their displays are noisy, elaborate and spectacular, involving much use of the expanded flank-plumes and including all sorts of posturing; it is in this genus that the famous 'hanging upside-down' displays are known. Males gather in large or medium-sized groups to display and within the general arena each has his own private display perch. These are all polygynous species. Interestingly one species, Goldie's Bird of Paradise, is confined to the D'Entrecasteaux Archipelago off eastern Papua New Guinea and from what is known of its habits seems to be a somewhat less advanced *Paradisaea* than its fellows on the mainland, which have presumably evolved at a faster rate in the face of more competition.

Bowerbirds

AS WITH THE BIRDS OF PARADISE, it is just possible that one or two bowerbirds remain undiscovered somewhere in New Guinea; one, the Yellow-fronted Gardener Bowerbird, is still totally unknown in the wild and another, Archbold's Bowerbird, was only discovered forty years ago. To date, eighteen species are recognized; nine are confined to New Guinea and seven to Australia, while two are common to both.

Although some are brilliantly coloured and others have brightly-coloured crests, most bowerbirds are relatively soberly dressed and all are generally similar in appearance – rather stocky birds with short and relatively stout bills. Most of them are essentially forest birds, but they are less arboreal and spend much more time on the ground than the birds of paradise; unlike the latter, a few species have moved out of woodland habitats into more open country, even including grassland with very sparse cover. Another important difference is that bowerbirds are mostly much more accomplished singers than birds of paradise, most of which have harsh and very unmusical voices; several species have almost ventriloquial voices and others are excellent mimics of other birds.

It is at once obvious that the birds of paradise have evolved an extraordinary range of ornamental plumages and bright colours to enable them to attract and secure their mates, whether this is done monogamously (as is the case with about 98 per cent of all perching birds) or polygynously and very temporarily. The bowerbirds have achieved something quite different, having in effect replaced their own physical appearance as a major attraction to females by the bowers which they build and decorate: they are unique among birds in this respect. Precisely how this curious form of behaviour evolved, and why, is far from clear, but it does seem likely that bowerbirds share a common ancestor with birds of paradise which, presumably, was something like the cnemophiline species we have described. Some birds of paradise already appear to be moving down from displaying in trees to doing so on or near the ground, where some even maintain cleared display courts. There is perhaps a link between this evolutionary trend and the behaviour of bowerbirds, which came to earth as it were long ago and have now set off on an evolutionary side-road of their own.

Several features are worthy of mention among these fascinating birds. Firstly, there is a broad generalization which can be made which states that the more brightly plumaged the male, the less elaborate in construction and ornamentation the bower. Similarly, there is an apparent correlation between vocal ability and plumage colour, the best vocalists being the least colourful. In addition, there is an interesting contrast between bowerbirds and birds of paradise where the most colourful part of the plumage occurs: generally speaking, this is on the undersurfaces on birds of paradise, most of which display from perches, often at a great height above the ground, but is on the upper surface (crests, capes etc) in bowerbirds, which display on the ground and must be seen by females from above.

The bowers themselves are constructed solely by the males. Each bower may be owned by a single bird, or, in some species, by several. There are four main types of construction. The simplest is a stage on the forest floor, merely an area cleared of debris and decorated with a few leaves, such as is built by the catbirds. Archbold's Bowerbird alone builds the second type, a mat-like stage of twigs and ferns. The third type is an avenue which comprises a long mat of twigs with side walls of vertical sticks (usually two, but four in one species), and this is built by the Regent Bowerbirds, the Satin Bowerbird and the four *Chlamydera* species. The fourth and most elaborate kind is the maypole bower built by the Gardener Bowerbirds and the Golden Bowerbird: this is a column of twigs around one or more saplings sometimes with a hut-like roof.

Most bowerbirds are polygynous and attract females by the construction and decoration of bowers and by the displays they perform there. Males may display singly or in loosely-spaced groups, in this respect resembling the birds of paradise which also use an arena system. It is generally accepted that bower-building originated as a form of displacement nest-building: a number of species of birds build nests to stimulate females as part of their general courtship behaviour (which may not be the nests ultimately used by her for laying in).

Decoration of the bower is an important

feature and here it is at once apparent that colour selection is employed by bowerbirds. Broadly speaking, the catbirds tend to select green or greenish objects (leaves), the avenue-builders colours in the green to violet range (black and blue berries for the Regent Bowerbirds, mainly bluish objects for the Satin Bowerbird and white bones and shells and green to bluish fruits and flowers for the *Chlamydera* group) and the maypole builders reds and yellows (berries and flowers for the Golden Bowerbird and flowers, fruits, fungi and bark for the Gardener Bowerbirds). Some species readily make use of all sorts of human debris (glass, tinfoil, paper etc) and one, the Great Grey Bowerbird, will even go so far as to steal small objects from man for this purpose. Probably the most extraordinary feature of bower-decoration is bower-painting, in which the birds apply a mixture of masticated vegetable matter and saliva to the bower walls. This unique habit is already known from a few species and may well prove common to more in due course.

The catbirds, so named for their loud, catlike calls, are monogamous birds of the dense substage of mountain forests and occur both in Australia and New Guinea. Their bower activity is of the simple stage kind, involving the maintenance of open courts with a few leaves for decoration. One species, the Tooth-billed Catbird, has a specially modified upper mandible with a distinct tooth which the male uses to strip leaves for his stage. Formerly placed in a separate genus (*Scenopoeetes*) this bird is now thought to be a valid member of the catbird genus *Ailuroedus*. Archbold's Bowerbird, in which the male is a striking black bird with a golden-yellow crest, is a species which, although discovered comparatively recently, has been well studied at its bower.

The four Gardener Bowerbirds of the genus *Amblyornis* include one wholly unknown species and two with a very limited distribution; all are confined to New Guinea. These are the builders of the maypole-type bowers, roofed over in two species, and all are splendid singers and mimics. The simplest bower, with its maypole and exposed display runway, is built by Macgregor's Gardener Bowerbird, a bird with a long orange crest; the Striped Gardener Bowerbird represents a midway stage between that species and the crestless and therefore least colourful Vogelkop Gardener Bowerbird, which compensates by building the most elaborate maypole bower of all. The Golden Bowerbird, an Australian species, builds a very complex bower despite its bright plumage.

The Regent Bowerbirds, two of which occur in New Guinea and one in Australia, all have brightly-coloured males and, broadly speaking, construct relatively simple bowers. It is thought that bower use may be rather sporadic among at least some of these birds (but not perhaps the Australian species) and that as a group they may be in the process of discarding bower behaviour altogether – and perhaps gaining more colourful plumage in compensation.

Another avenue-builder, the Satin Bowerbird of Australia, builds a rather simple but nevertheless elaborately decorated (and painted) bower. It is a polygynous species, with traditional courtship areas in which groups of males display, each with his own private court and bower. Finally, the four *Chlamydera* species are interesting in that some of them have extended the range of bowerbirds out into open country; one of them, the Great Grey, enjoys something of a reputation in parts of Australia – as a thief. The basically dull plumage of these bowerbirds no doubt has some function as cryptic coloration in open grassland habitats, but it is probably also related to bower-building: these birds probably derived from Regent Bowerbird stock, but have lost all but a remnant of the bright plumage and have instead developed the most elaborate and elaborately decorated types of avenue bowers. One species, Lauterbach's Bowerbird, is unique in having four walls to its bower instead of the usual two.

Hybrids

FINALLY, A WORD SHOULD BE SAID on the subject of hybrid birds of paradise and bowerbirds. Hybridization does occur in a few cases where bird of paradise species meet one another at a point of range overlap in New Guinea (e.g. between Count Raggi's and the Lesser Birds of Paradise), but of more interest to us here is the existence of a number of so-called rare birds of paradise named from specimens which turned up during the heyday of the plumage trade in Europe. For many years it was believed that these must have been evidence of rare and undiscovered species existing in the remoter parts of New Guinea, but it is now thought that all are actually hybrids.

All the known hybrids are listed, with their original scientific names, in Gilliard's book – thirteen between different genera of birds of paradise, one between different genera of bowerbirds and five between birds of paradise of a common genus. We have already hinted that in view of the comparatively recent discovery of two new species, the existence of another which nobody has ever succeeded in finding in the wild, and the continuing inaccessibility of parts of New Guinea, one or two new species may still remain to be discovered.

Loria's Bird of Paradise
Loria loriae

Distribution: New Guinea, more or less throughout the mountains but apparently not the Vogelkop and Huon peninsulas; usually from 1800 to 2700 m (*6000 to 9000 ft*), less commonly down to 1500 m (*5000 ft*).

Description: 200–230 mm (*8–9 in*). This is a relatively stocky, short-tailed and stout-billed species. Males are almost uniformly velvety-black with the forehead and lores iridescent blue-green and the secondaries glossed with blue or purple. The narrow gape-wattles at the base of the bill are whitish-yellow. In contrast, the female is more or less yellow-green all over, slightly paler on the underparts, and with a somewhat scaly appearance to the upperparts caused by faint dark margins to the feathers. Her wings and tail are noticeably browner.

Breeding: So far, the nest and eggs have not been described. Nor has the display, although males apparently move around a very small area high in a tree repeating their bell-like calls at long intervals.

Remarks: These birds are commonly heard in the higher forests of central New Guinea and their calls have a strongly ventriloquial quality unknown in other birds of paradise. Except when calling (and possibly displaying) in this way, the birds are usually seen at no great height above the ground. As far as is known, the diet is wholly fruit.

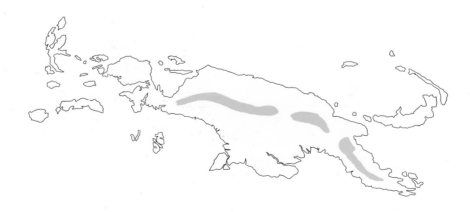

Loria's Bird of Paradise

Loria loriae

Wattle-billed Bird of Paradise
Loboparadisea sericea

Distribution: New Guinea, between 1200 and 1900 m (*4000 and 6200 ft*), from Weyland to the Herzog Mountains.

Description: 160–180 mm (*6½–7 in*). This is a very distinctive species, roughly starling-sized with yellow and brown plumage. There are two well-marked races: in the western part of the range, males have the crown, ear-coverts and nape dark brown, grading into dark reddish-brown washed with gold on the upper back, while the lower back and rump are pale yellow. The underparts are pale yellow, the wings and tail chestnut-brown. Eastern birds have rather more yellowish-brown upperparts and the upper back olive-yellow and are greener on the crown. Thick yellow wattles at the base of the bill are unique to this species. Females resemble males but lack the wattles, have dark olive-brown upperparts and largely brown rumps and are duller below.

Breeding: The nest and eggs of this little-known species have yet to be described, as has its display, but natives say nests are open and made of grass, placed on a low branch, and that one egg is laid.

Remarks: Apparently this is a quiet, rather inactive species, usually encountered at no great height above the ground in the underbrush. It seems to be solely a fruit-eater.

Wattle-billed Bird of Paradise

Loboparadisea sericea

Sickle-crested Bird of Paradise

Cnemophilus macgregorii

Distribution: New Guinea, from 2300 to 3400 m (*7600 to 11,000 ft*) in the east and south-east.

Description: 250 mm (*9¾ in*). The male is orange-red above, shading to a paler, browner orange on the lower back and tail, although one subspecies is more golden-yellow above, shading to yellowish-brown, and with a little red on the crown. The inner secondaries and wing-coverts are yellowish-brown and the underparts are wholly dark blackish-brown. The unique crest on the forehead is composed of between four and six narrow olive or reddish-brown plumes, tinged with violet. Females are very different, being dark olive-brown above, slightly scaled in appearance, with brownish wings and tail and olive- or buffish-brown underparts.

Breeding: A single white egg, irregularly ringed with dark spots at its larger end and with a few more spots on its surface, is laid in a domed nest quite unlike those of other birds of paradise. Built of moss, ferns and small roots and lined with dead leaves and feathers, it is a soft, thick structure and is apparently typically placed in a hole in a rotten stump only a few metres above the ground. The male has a variety of calls, the most curious of which has been described as 'the sound of two timbers being rubbed together under considerable stress', but so far no displays have been described.

Remarks: Until its nest was found twenty years ago this was believed to be a species of bowerbird; it is now known to be quite closely related to the two preceding species of birds of paradise. It is a shy, elusive species of lower forest and undergrowth and is apparently rare except at high altitudes.

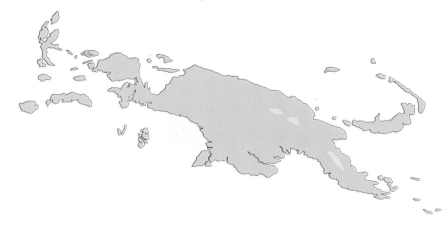

Sickle-crested Bird of Paradise

Cnemophilus macgregorii

Macgregor's Bird of Paradise

Macgregoria pulchra

Macgregor's Bird of Paradise

Macgregoria pulchra

Distribution: New Guinea, from 2700 to 4000 m (*9000 to 13,000 ft*) in the western and south-eastern parts of the island: also found recently in central New Guinea.

Description: 380–400 mm (*15–16 in*). Both sexes are alike, the male being slightly larger than the female. The plumage is entirely velvet-black, relieved only by the yellowish-orange primaries, themselves tipped black, and the very large orange lappet wattles around the eye and over the ear-coverts.

Breeding: Monogamous. Active courtship chases, involving two or more birds, take place in the treetops, the birds flying noisily around a large area and hopping from branch to branch, often pausing to rest and preen. Clicking calls are uttered from time to time. A bulky nest is built 11 to 15 m (*35 to 50 ft*) above the ground, usually in a Podocarpus tree, and a single earthy-pink egg is laid.

Remarks: This species is named after its discoverer, Sir William Macgregor, a pioneer administrator of Papua in the 19th century. It is a common, conspicuous species of high altitude pine forests, occurring right up to the limits of tree growth, and is active and not at all shy. Single birds are not often seen, the birds usually travelling in pairs or small flocks. Its food is believed to be entirely tree fruits.

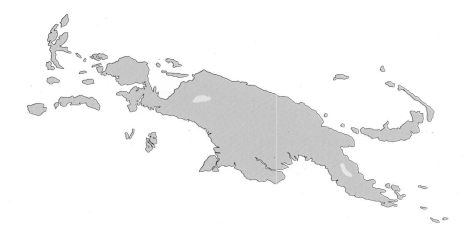

Paradise or Silky Crow

Lucocorax pyrrhopterus

Paradise or Silky Crow
Lycocorax pyrrhopterus

Distribution: Confined to the islands of the Moluccan ar-chipelago where it occurs from sea–level up to 1600 m (*5200 ft*).

Description: 355–430 mm (*14–17 in*). This little-known species is superficially crow-like, being all-dark, apart from buffish-white tinges on the inner flight-feathers and a crimson eye. At close quarters, the plumage is a dusky brownish or blackish colour, with a slight greenish gloss, and is rather duller on the wings. The tail is dark bluish-black. The sexes are alike, but the female is a little smaller than the male.

Breeding: Monogamous. A large, basin-shaped nest is built, roughly 6 to 8 m (*20 to 25 ft*) above the ground and in this one egg is laid, pinkish in colour with fine lines and hairstreaks of brown, violet and black.

Remarks: Although this is a fairly common bird in the man-grove edge and hill forests of the Moluccas, it is rather shy and difficult to observe. It is probably easier to hear than to see, being an active and highly mobile bird which makes a whirring noise in flight and has one very distinctive call – likened by observers to a short bark from a rather hoarse dog. It feeds on fruits, especially those of the Pinang Palm.

Glossy-mantled Manucode
Manucodia ater

Distribution: New Guinea and adjacent islands – the Western Papuan Islands, Geelvink Bay islands and islands off the south-eastern coast. A lowland species, found from sea-level up to 900 m (*3000 ft*).

Description: 340–400 mm (*13½–16 in*). This species is all black, glossed with blue, green and purple, especially on the upperparts. The underparts are slightly duller and have a somewhat scalloped appearance. Males and females are alike, though the male is slightly larger.

Breeding: Monogamous. The only display described so far involves the male in spreading and shaking his wings and tail and fluffing out his body feathers. Nests are built 6 to 8 m (*20 to 25 ft*) up, either on a side-branch or in a complex of forked branches, and form a neat cup of coiled sticks and vines, lined with leaves, small stems and rotten wood. Two eggs are laid, which are greyish with pale brown spots and smudges and sometimes darker brown lines.

Remarks: This is a common species, apparently not particularly wary of man, found in the lower parts of the forest or in the tops of smaller trees. It feeds on fruit and is usually seen in pairs. In flight, the wings make a distinctive heavy rustling sound.

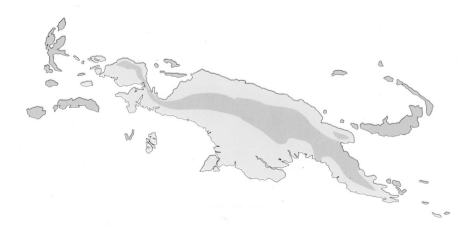

Glossy-mantled Manucode

Manucodia ater

Jobi Manucode
Manucodia jobiensis

Distribution: New Guinea – Japen Island and the lower part of northern New Guinea from Geelvink Bay east to the Astrolabe Bay area. A lowland bird, not found much above 500 m (*1600 ft*).

Description: 305–370 mm (*12–14½ in*). This bird closely resembles the Crinkle-collared Manucode, being all black and glossed with greenish-blue. The feathers of the head and neck are very short, slightly crinkled and glossed with green or purple (compare with the next species) and the Jobi Manucode has a rather shorter tail and finer bill than the Crinkle-collared. The sexes are alike, with the female slightly smaller than the male.

Breeding: Monogamous. The display has not so far been described. The nest is suspended between two branches and is deeply cup-shaped and made of roots, creepers and leaves. Two eggs are laid, pale pinkish with small brown spots and larger lavender-grey spots, mainly at the larger end.

Remarks: Although it is clearly a common lowland forest species, little is known of the life and habits of this manucode. It feeds on fruits and has a long, moaning call. Interestingly, it occurs alongside the almost indistinguishable Crinkle-collared Manucode and seems to differ from it only in behaviour.

Jobi Manucode

Manucodia jobiensis

Crinkle-collared Manucode

Manucodia chalybatus

Distribution: New Guinea and Misol Island, mainly from about 600 to 1700 m (*1900 to 5500 ft*), but also occasionally down to sea-level.

Description: 320–360 mm (*12¾–14¼ in*). Almost identical to the Jobi Manucode, this species is also all black with a greenish-blue and purplish gloss, but the short feathers on the neck and upper breast are more heavily crinkled and are tinged with metallic yellowish-green. Again, the sexes are alike, with the male being slightly the larger of the two.

Breeding: Monogamous. So far, no display has been described for this species. The nest resembles that of an oriole and is hung in the fork of a branch; it is made of stalks and leaves, lined with finer materials. Two eggs are laid, rather rounded in shape and creamy-white with brown and purplish-grey markings.

Remarks: Although this too is a widespread and apparently fairly common bird, very little is known of its life-history and habits.

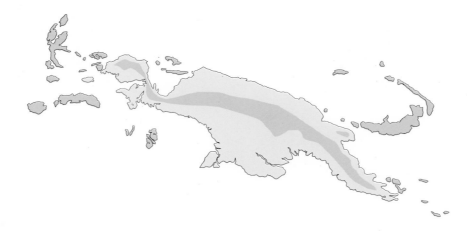

Crinkle-collared Manucode

Manucodia chalybatus

Curl-crested Manucode

Manucodia comrii

Distribution: Confined to the Trobriands and the D'Entrecasteaux Archipelago in the Eastern Papuan Islands.

Description: 445 mm (*17½ in*). This is the most distinctive of the manucodes, with its obvious curly crest and curiously twisted tail. Both sexes are alike (the female being slightly smaller) and are all black, with the short curled feathers of the crown showing a purple gloss, the curled and crinkled breast feathers glossed green and most of the upperparts glossed green or purple. The central tail-feathers are recurved and twisted, giving the tail a very distinctive appearance.

Breeding: Monogamous. So far, this species' display has not been described. Here too the nest is oriole-like, hung in the fork of a branch and built of twigs and vines, ornamented on the outside with large thick leaves. Two eggs are laid, pale salmon-buff or greyish-buff, with cinnamon, brown and grey spots and blotches.

Remarks: Very little is known of this interesting bird, except that it is apparently not uncommon within its restricted range. The plumes of this bird often feature in native ceremonies in the Trobriand Islands.

Curl-crested Manucode

Manucodia comrii

Trumpet Bird or Trumpet Manucode

Manucodia keraudrenii

Trumpet Bird or Trumpet Manucode
Manucodia keraudrenii

Distribution: New Guinea – lowlands up to 1800 m (*6000 ft*), also the Aru and D'Entrecasteaux Archipelagos; north-eastern Australia.

Description: 250–320 mm (*10–12½ in*). Although the Trumpet Bird is blackish in general appearance, it is variously glossed in a range of blues, greens and purples, with minor variations. Its most striking features are two elongated, pointed plumes on either side of the crown. As with other manucodes, the sexes are alike, the male being slightly larger than the female.

Breeding: Apparently monogamous. In display, the male chases the female through the trees, stopping to perform a display about a foot from her in which he raises and spreads his wings, erects his body feathers and calls once – a loud, trumpeting squawk from which it takes its name. The nest is an open, rather shallow cup placed in a high tree fork – up to 20 m (*70 ft*) high in Australia – and built largely of vines. Two eggs are laid, pale pinkish-purple streaked and blotched with brown, purple and grey.

Remarks: The call of the male is produced via an extremely long and coiled trachea extending from the throat down over the breast muscles. This very active species is common in rain-forest country in parts of New Guinea, occurring both low in the canopy and in the treetops, but is apparently shy and rather difficult to observe. As well as fruits and berries it also feeds on insects.

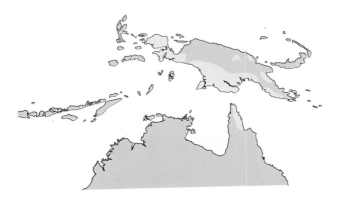

Paradise Riflebird
Ptiloris paradiseus

Distribution: Confined to eastern Australia, from the Hunter River area of New South Wales to central Queensland.

Description: 270 mm (*11 in*). This is a short-tailed species with a long, decurved bill in which the sexes are very different in appearance. The male is velvet-black, glossed purplish-green on the crown, throat, foreneck and central tail-feathers, the metallic green on the throat and breast forming a distinct 'shield' with erectile feathers at the sides. The lower breast and belly are broadly tipped with olive-green. The female is largely grey-brown above, with the crown and sides of the neck darker, a whitish superciliary stripe and broad rufous edges to the wing- and tail-feathers. Her whitish-buff throat grades into more buffish underparts which are well marked with dark chevrons.

Breeding: Monogamous. After flying round and calling in the treetops (a long-drawn 'ya-a-ass') the male descends to a lower, exposed bare branch to display: with his head thrown back and his wings extended, he whirls round and round, first one way, then the other. The nest is a shallow bowl, made of leaves, vines, fibres and twigs and often ornamented with sloughed-off snake skins. Two eggs are laid, cream in colour and spotted and streaked with chestnut, purple and grey.

Remarks: This is an uncommon bird of rain-forest country, often found in the lower stratum of the forest where it feeds on insects which it probes for with its long bill around and under the bark of tree-trunks and logs; as it moves from tree to tree, its feathers produce a distinctive silky, rustling sound. Its name apparently derives from the resemblance of its plumage to the dark uniforms of 19th-century British riflemen.

Paradise Riflebird

Ptiloris paradiseus

Queen Victoria or Victoria Riflebird

Ptiloris victoriae

Distribution: Australia, confined to the Cairns district of northern Queensland.

Description: 220 mm ($8\frac{3}{4}$ in). This species resembles the Paradise Riflebird very closely, but is somewhat smaller. In addition, the olive-green tips to the lower breast and belly feathers present in both species are broader in the Victoria Riflebird and totally conceal the broad black bases of the feathers. The female is a richer, cinnamon brown on the underparts which are marked with fewer dark chevrons.

Breeding: Monogamous. The nest is similar to that of the Paradise Riflebird and is likewise often decorated with snake skins. Two eggs are laid, dark flesh-colour with red, brown and purple streaks and smudges. Males are apparently strongly territorial and have traditional display perches — bare, exposed branches or large stumps. They visit each perch in turn, pausing to emit a rough, loud 'ya-a-rr' call, and then go through a full display. Pairs have been seen performing extraordinary displays together, in which they face each other, breasts almost touching, each bird in turn slowly stretching upwards, raising its wings horizontally and sweeping them slightly forward, all the while increasing the tempo until their heads are thrown further and further back and their gaping bills are opened wider and wider. At the climax, when both birds quiver all over, their tails are spread and the wings are thrown forward in front of the breast and are rocked sideways and up-and-down.

Remarks: Like the Paradise Riflebird, this is an extremely agile feeder on tree-trunks and stumps, seeking out insects below the bark with its long, fine bill. It also feeds on the ground, and eats forest fruits.

Queen Victoria or Victoria Riflebird

Ptiloris victoriae

Magnificent Riflebird

Ptiloris magnificus

Magnificent Riflebird
Ptiloris magnificus

Distribution: Common and widespread in New Guinea and north-eastern Australia, from sea-level to 1200 m (*4000 ft*).

Description: 330 mm (*13 in*). This species resembles the two preceding riflebirds, but is fractionally bigger than the Paradise. The male has a much more extensive erectile, fan-like shield on the throat and breast, iridescent purple-green in colour and separated from the dull purplish belly by two bands of velvet-black and olive-green. The feathers of the flanks extend into long, filamentous plumes. Females are cinnamon-brown above, redder on the tail, with a broad black streak along the side of the throat and buffish-white underparts with blackish-brown speckles on the upper breast and bars on the lower breast and belly.

Breeding: Monogamous. The nest is a cup of vines, leaves and fine fibrous material, often at no great height above the ground, in which two eggs are laid – creamish with brown and grey streaks. Two fairly distinct forms of display have been described; in a short display, the male throws his wings slightly forward, extends them fully, stretches his neck to show his breast-shield fully and moves his head very rapidly and rhythmically from side to side; in the longer display he opens his wings so rapidly that a sharp 'plop' is heard, after which he rhythmically moves his head from side to side, raising his body and relaxing his fully-opened wings as he does so, and as the head reaches far to one side the wings close as rapidly as they opened.

Remarks: A fairly common bird, this species is very similar in its habits to the two previous species.

Wallace's Standard Wing

Semioptera wallacei

Distribution: Confined to the Moluccan islands of Halmahera and Batjan.

Description: 250 mm (*10 in*). The male of this extraordinary-looking bird is basically a rather pale brown in colour, darker on the upperparts and greyer on the flight-feathers, glossed with various shades of lilac, purple and green. His most striking features are a vividly iridescent green breast shield, suffused with gold and greatly elongated at the sides, a slight crest and a yellowish tuft of feathers at the base of the upper mandible and a pair of incredibly long white pennants or plumes extending from the bend of the wing. The female resembles the male, but lacks his long plumes and green gloss and has the nasal tuft paler and more buff in colour.

Breeding: The details of breeding are largely unknown, but it is apparent that males display communally in 'arenas' and band together apart from females, so it is reasonable to suppose that this is a polygamous species. In displaying, males raise their breast shields perpendicularly and the long pennants on the wings are extended outwards at right-angles below them and are constantly raised and depressed. The crown feathers are also erected.

Remarks: Relatively little is known about this remarkable bird, the best description of it still being that of A. R. Wallace, who discovered it in 1858 on Batjan, and W. Goodfellow, who watched it on Halmahera in 1926. It is clearly a gregarious bird, not confined to densely wooded country, and is an active and highly mobile species. As well as fruits, it apparently eats a wide variety of insects.

Wallace's Standard Wing

Semioptera wallacei

Twelve-wired Bird of Paradise

Seleucidis melanoleuca

Twelve-wired Bird of Paradise

Seleucidis melanoleuca

Distribution: Salawati (Western Papuan Islands) and New Guinea, except the north coast of the eastern end, in lowland forests near sea-level.

Description: 320–340 mm (*12½–13½ in*). The male is a handsome black-and-yellow bird with a long bill. His head and upperparts are velvety black, glossed with purple and green, while the breast is black tinged with green. The feathers of the upper breast are long and when erected form a breast-shield edged with iridescent emerald. The underparts are pale yellow, with very long ornamental plumes on either side of the breast; six plumes on each side are lengthened into dark, wire-like projections up to 290 mm (*11¼ in*) long. The female is chestnut above and greyish below, the whole underside being closely barred with brown. Her pale throat contrasts with a distinctive black cap and nape.

Breeding: Probably polygamous. In display, which is from a high, exposed branch, the male extends his breast-shield, compressing the body plumage to make the shield as obvious as possible; when this happens, the elongated plumes on the flanks are expanded and the twelve wires align themselves in such a way that they extend forward and around and beneath the body. He will also whirl around a vertical branch and open and close his wings ten to twelve times, with great rapidity, uttering sharp metallic calls. The nest is a rather shallow cup of vines and bark strippings on a scanty base of sticks and leaves, in which one egg is laid, creamish with reddish and grey streaking, especially at the larger end.

Remarks: This is a rather shy and uncommon species of lowland forests and swamps and its habits and social organization are little known. Males have been seen in small groups.

Long-tailed Paradigalla
Paradigalla carunculata

Distribution: New Guinea, between 1500 and 2100 m (*4800 and 7000 ft*) in the Arfak and western Snow mountain ranges.

Description: 355–380 mm (*14–15 in*). The male Long-tailed Paradigalla is basically all black, glossed with blue and green and, in some lights, deep bronze. Its crown and nape are especially glossy, with scale-like blue and green feathers. The tail is fairly long and in one of the two subspecies is distinctly wedge-shaped. Between the base of the bill and the eye there is a large yellow or greenish-yellow wattle, with some red at its outer edges, and a smaller wattle at the base of the lower mandible is blue and orange-yellow or lemon yellow. Females are very like males but are rather duller and blacker and slightly smaller with less well-developed wattles.

Breeding: Nothing is known.

Remarks: Very little is known of this elusive bird, except that it eats fruit and is found in mountain forest.

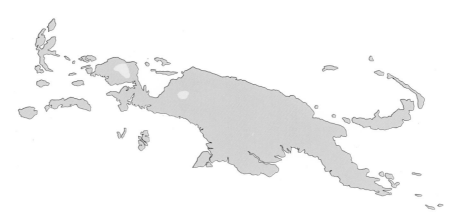

Long-tailed Paradigalla

Paradigalla carunculata

Short-tailed Paradigalla
Paradigalla brevicauda

Distribution: New Guinea, in the central mountain ranges from 1700 to 2400 m (*5500 to 7800 ft*).

Description: 215–250 mm (*8½–9 in*). The male Short-tailed Paradigalla is a rather stocky, slender–billed bird, black all over with a slight bronze gloss to the upperparts and breast and a bronze-green gloss on the wing-feathers. The blue-green gloss on the cap is particularly prominent and in front of each eye there is a bright yellow erectile wattle with a smaller bright blue and yellow one at the base of the lower mandible. Females resemble males closely but are duller black and have smaller wattles.

Breeding: This is completely unknown.

Remarks: Although this seems to be a fairly common species, at least in some parts of its range, little is known of its habits in the wild and its nest has been only vaguely described. It occurs in pure forest and is apparently usually seen in the crowns of extremely high mature trees; its food is said to be mainly seeds and small fruits.

Short-tailed Paradigalla

Paradigalla brevicauda

Black-billed Sickle-billed Bird of Paradise

Drepanornis albertisii

Distribution: New Guinea, where it is numerous in mountains from 600 to 2200 m (*2000 to 7200 ft*).

Description: 355 mm (*14 in*). The male is rusty brown above, more chestnut on the rump and tail, and more or less sooty-brown below with a black line across the lower breast. There are naked patches of blue skin on the sides of the head and in front of the eyes iridescent black feathers project as small 'horns'. At the sides of the breast are long tufts (65 mm/*2½ in*) of darker feathers, while even longer tufts (100 mm/*4 in*) on the flanks are dark brown and tipped with purple. The female is rather different, being brown above like the male but lacking the iridescent feathers in front of the eye and the erectile tufts; her underparts are buffish with fine, darker barring.

Breeding: The display of this bird has not been described, but presumably involves the spreading of the breast and flank tufts. Little is known of its breeding habits, except that the nest is a shallow affair built in the horizontal fork of a branch, made of fine roots and grasses. One egg is laid, creamy with a reddish tinge and spotted and streaked with brown and grey, especially at the larger end.

Remarks: Very little is known about this elusive bird, possibly because it appears to spend much of its life in the uppermost branches of the tallest trees. The long, fine bill is probably used in seeking out insects on dead trees and tree-trunks, but this has not been confirmed.

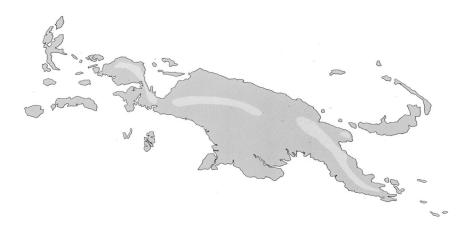

Black-billed Sickle-billed Bird of Paradise

Drepanornis albertisii

White-billed Sickle-billed Bird of Paradise
Drepanornis bruijnii

Distribution: North-west New Guinea, in the lowlands from Geelvink Bay to the Humboldt Bay area.

Description: 340 mm (*13½ in*). There is a close resemblance between this bird and the preceding species, although in *Drepanornis bruijnii* the long, finely curved bill is whitish. Again, the male's upperparts are dark brown, but chestnut on the crown and tail and more reddish-brown on the wings; above the eye the short feathers have a purple gloss and black tips. The throat and ear-coverts are black and there is an iridescent purple spot below the eye. Two tufts of feathers on the dark lower throat are black with a brilliant copper-coloured band near their tips, while the underparts are grey. The longest feathers on the sides of the underparts are tipped with black and bluish-purple and a shorter series have a green gloss. Females are like males, except that they lack the black on the head and the ornamental tufts and have buffish underparts barred with black.

Breeding: Nothing is known of this bird's display or its breeding habits.

Remarks: This is a very localized species and remains largely unknown to ornithologists. Some calls have been described – a series of loud descending whistles, repeated again and again, and various gruff, churring noises.

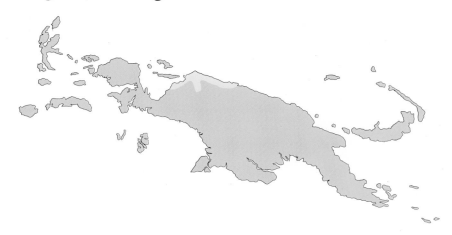

White-billed Sickle-billed Bird of Paradise

Drepanornis bruijnii

Black Sickle-billed Bird of Paradise
Epimachus fastosus

Distribution: New Guinea, in forests of the western and central area, from 1300 to 2300 m (*4200 to 7700 ft*).

Description: 1120 mm (*44 in*) – including tail of about 840 mm (*33 in*). The striking-looking male of this species is virtually all black, with copper, blue and green iridescences and an extremely long tail, black glossed with purplish blue. His bill is long and decurved and at each side of the upper breast there is a large green and violet glossed fan of feathers, with a larger velvet-black fan behind it. A third fan extends from the sides of the lower breast. Beside the bizarre male, the female is much less spectacular, being olive-brown above, with a dark chestnut crown, and blackish on the throat and breast, below which the lower underparts are greyish with narrower black bars.

Breeding: The nest and eggs are unknown, but one display by the male has been described: the bird sits on a high, bare branch, with all the breast fans spread outwards and upwards, rather like raised arms, and the tail partly spread so that the short outer feathers show quite clearly. After uttering a loud, penetrating whistle, it dives from the branch with spread wings and then sails back up to the same perch.

Remarks: This is not an uncommon species, although little is known about it. It has very distinctive loud, liquid, whip-like calls and is known to eat various fruits.

Black Sickle-billed Bird of Paradise

Epimachus fastosus

Brown Sickle-billed Bird of Paradise
Epimachus meyeri

Distribution: New Guinea, from 1600 to 3000 m (*5400 to 10,000 ft*), from the Weyland and Snow Mountains to the south-eastern part of the island.

Description: 990 mm (*39 in*), including very long tail. The male of this species is very similar to that of *Epimachus fastosus*, being black above, glossed with green, blue and purple, with a long curved bill and a very long tail, but its underparts are dull olive-brown, paler towards the abdomen and tinged with purple at the sides. At the side of the upper breast is a large fan of dark feathers, some tipped with violet, with long sooty plumes behind. A second grey- or white-tipped breast fan lies below this one, some of its feathers forming long, fine plumes reaching beyond the base of the tail. In contrast, the female is brownish above, tinged chestnut on the back and yellowish-chestnut on the crown, with a dark sooty throat and pale buff underparts barred with black and brown.

Breeding: Polygamous. A cup-shaped nest of moss and vines, lined with fine roots and leaves, is attached to slender branches or a small fork in a tree. One egg is laid, cinnamon with brown and reddish streaks at the larger end and brown and lavender spots elsewhere. In one form of display, the male draws his body erect, with the tail slightly spread and the flank plumes widely spread; the breast fans are thrown upwards, almost hiding the head, and the beak is opened to show its bright yellow interior. Sometimes the bird jerkily rotates its body this way and that.

Remarks: This bird probes for insects and tree frogs with its long bill, but also eats fruits. Its call (which the male uses in some of his displays) was described by Gilliard as 'a loud clatter sounding very much like a pneumatic hammer'. Its long tail-plumes are much prized by natives.

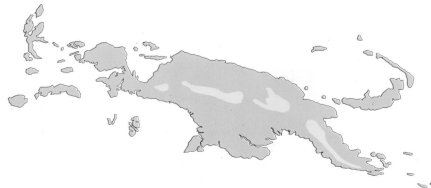

Brown Sickle-billed Bird of Paradise

Epimachus meyeri

Arfak Astrapia Bird of Paradise

Astrapia nigra

Distribution: New Guinea, confined to the Arfak Mountains from 1600 to 2200 m (*5400 to 7100 ft*).

Description: 735–800 mm (*29–31½ in*). The male is basically a black bird with a very long tail, with various iridescences, especially on the hind neck where there is an erectile fan of brilliant green, and long feathers of a brilliant coppery hue forming a border to the sides of the breast and meeting in a narrow band across the breast. Females are more or less brown above, with the throat and upper breast blackish–brown and the underparts blackish with narrow buff bars.

Breeding: The nest and eggs are unknown, as are the displays, but it is thought that males use display arenas and are polygamous.

Remarks: This magnificent bird (appropriately described as 'L'Incomparable' by the French ornithologist Levaillant) has a very restricted distribution in particularly difficult country, where it lives in the treetops in mountain forests. Its life history is almost wholly unknown.

Arfak Astrapia Bird of Paradise

Astrapia nigra

Splendid Astrapia Bird of Paradise
Astrapia splendidissima

Distribution: New Guinea, between 1800 and 3000 m (*5800 and 10,000 ft*) in the Snow Mountains, from Weyland and Nassau east to the Hindenburg and Victor Emanuel mountains.

Description: 430 mm (*17 in*), including tail of 200–230 mm (*8–9 in*). The male is basically black, glossed with purple, but with the head an iridescent yellowish-green, the nape feathers lengthening to form an iridescent blue-green cape, tinged with purple, and with white central tail-feathers. A blue-black band borders the green throat, the whole bordered by a coppery red band which joins a similar, broader band across the breast. Females are blackish-brown above and black from the head and neck down onto the breast, with buffish underparts and rather less white on the tail than in the male.

Breeding: The breeding system is unknown, but males probably live apart from females and are presumably polygamous. No displays are known, but it seems likely that they are of the arena type. The cape on the hind-neck is no doubt spread in display.

Remarks: This *Astrapia* is as little known as the preceding species; it is apparently a fairly common bird but is shy and elusive. It has been watched feeding on insects among branches and vines and is also known to eat tree frogs, lizards and various fruits.

Splendid Astrapia Bird of Paradise

Astrapia splendidissima

Ribbon-tailed Bird of Paradise

Astrapia mayeri

Ribbon-tailed Bird of Paradise
Astrapia mayeri

Distribution: New Guinea, but restricted to a small area in the Central Highlands on Mt Giluwe and Mt Hagen and for perhaps 125 km (*80 miles*) westwards; occurs from 2400 to 3000 m (*7800 to 10,000 ft*).

Description: 1170 mm (*46 in*), including extremely long tail (up to 920 mm/*36 in*). Like the other Astrapia males, the Ribbon-tailed male is a black bird, glossed with bronze-green on the upperparts, purple on the head and copper and green on the underparts. There is a large green tuft of feathers at the base of the bill, half concealing the upper mandible, and a cape of black, glossed purple, from the nape onto the upper back. A coppery breast band lies below the glossy blue-green throat. The most striking feature is the immensely long tail – or rather its two narrow, much elongated, virtually all white central tail-feathers. The female is black above, with browner wings and tail, the latter sometimes with some white, black on the breast and barred buffish-brown and black on the lower underparts. She has iridescent green feathers on the crown and nape.

Breeding: Presumably polygamous. The nest is a shallow cup of vines, mosses and leaves, but so far the egg has not been described. The full display of the male is unknown, but partial displays include drooping the wings and raising them high above the back and twitching the long tail from side to side. Presumably the cape is raised and expanded in some displays.

Remarks: Discovered as recently as 1939, this is a common species within its restricted range, where it feeds in the upper parts of forest trees, crawling and climbing on branches and eating fruits. It meets the Princess Stephanie Bird of Paradise in the extreme eastern part of its range and hybridization occurs.

Princess Stephanie Bird of Paradise
Astrapia stephaniae

Distribution: New Guinea, from the south-east west to Mt Hagen, between 1500 and 2700 m (*5000 and 9000 ft*).

Description: 760–840 mm (*30–33 in*), including very long tail. The male is another mainly black Astrapia, with greenish iridescence on the upperparts, and with the head and much of the upper breast glossy yellowish-green tinged with blue. Below this area there is a black breast band, with bronze iridescence, and below that a band of gleaming copper red. The long broad tail is black with pinkish-purple reflections and white feather shafts. Females are much duller, being largely brown and black on the back, buff with dark bars below, and black on the head and breast.

Breeding: Presumably polygamous. The nest is a thick, shallow cup of leaves and creepers, lined with fine roots, placed high in a forest tree; one egg is laid, pale brown with brown streaks and, at the larger end, a few red-brown spots. Males display high above the ground and in one display a male was seen holding the tail down in an inverted V, with the wings held over the back in such a way that the carpal joints almost met above the back and the primaries extended outwards at right angles to the body; the head was inclined downwards and the neck held in a crook-shaped position.

Remarks: This is a common bird of high mountain forests where it apparently subsists largely on fruit, although insects have also been recorded in its diet. Like the other Astrapias, it sports tail-feathers much used by natives for decoration. It was named in 1884 for the Crown Princess of Austria.

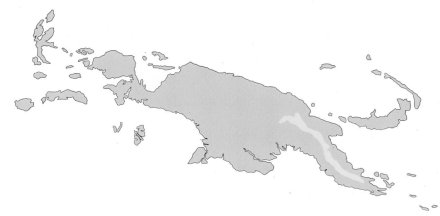

Princess Stephanie Bird of Paradise

Astrapia stephaniae

Huon Astrapia Bird of Paradise

Astrapia rothschildi

Huon Astrapia Bird of Paradise
Astrapia rothschildi

Distribution: New Guinea, confined to the mountains of the Huon Peninsula from 1500 to 2300 m (*4800 to 7500 ft*).

Description: 635 mm (*25 in*), including tail (330 mm / *13 in*). Males are black, glossed blue on the crown and coppery on the nape, with purple and green tips to the elongated nape feathers; the back is distinctly tinged greenish-bronze and the long, broad tail with purple. There is a narrow coppery-bronze breast band below the elongated black and blue-glossed breast feathers and the remaining underparts are dark green. Females have black heads and breasts, largely brown upperparts and black underparts with fine whitish bars.

Breeding: Presumably polygamous. The nest is unknown, but one egg has been described – pinkish in colour with brown blotches at the larger end and grey streaks overall. Two displays have been described: in one, a male stood erect with his tail tipped forward and partly spread, with the blue-glossed feathers of the breast spread and flattened into a shield, exposing golden-copper edges to the feathers, and with the greenish breast-feathers expanded. In the other display, the male tipped backwards and hung upside-down, with the head and tail both directed upward; the breast-shield was spread, as were the feathers of the abdomen, while the ear-coverts were opened to form a ruff on the nape. The wings were tightly closed, but the back feathers were extended sideways over them. The tail, at first opened widely, was then rapidly opened and closed.

Remarks: The above displays were recorded from captive males. Virtually nothing is known of this species in the wild.

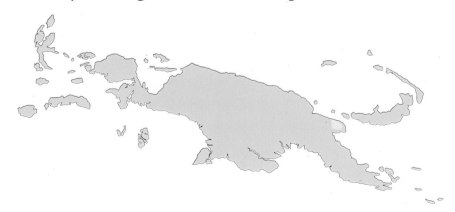

Superb Bird of Paradise
Lophorina superba

Distribution: New Guinea, virtually throughout, from 1000 to 2200 m (*3200 to 7250 ft*).

Description: 215–250 mm (*8½–10 in*). The male is an extraordinary-looking bird, largely black with an iridescent blue-green to purplish crown and a bronze throat, but with a large, erectile breast-shield of iridescent green and an enormous cape of black feathers with bronze reflections. This cape extends mainly from the rear of the head and is normally carried over the back, but it is fully erectile. The very different female occurs in two distinct forms, both lacking the ornamental feathers of the male; the upperparts are either deep reddish-brown or greyish-brown, the head black or dark brown with white on the forehead and broad white superciliary stripes, and the underparts greyish with narrow dark bars.

Breeding: Polygamous. Surprisingly, perhaps, for such a widespread and common bird, its breeding behaviour is hardly known at all. The nest is a shallow cup of twigs, leaves and fine roots, placed in a tree fork, in which two eggs are laid, buffish to creamy in colour, streaked and spotted with brown, grey and rufous. Males display on large branches in the lower canopy, but what actually happens has only been described from captive birds: the male crouches on a perch, partly opens his wings and fully spreads his breast shield, also erecting his fantastic cape until it surrounds his head like a huge ruff. He then dances clumsily, now and then emitting thin, harsh screams and showing his bright yellow mouth.

Remarks: This species is often seen feeding on fruits at the forest edge and in secondary growth; insects are also taken.

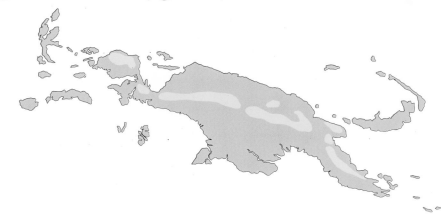

Superb Bird of Paradise

Lophorina superba

Wahnes' Six-wired Bird of Paradise

Parotia wahnesi

Distribution: New Guinea, confined to the Huon Peninsula, from 1200 to 1700 m (*3800 to 5500 ft*).

Description: 410–445 mm (*16–17½ in*). The noticeably long-tailed male is all black, with an erectile gold tuft on the forehead, a patch of iridescent violet on the nape, a large, iridescent yellowish-green breast shield and some purple glossing on the throat and neck. The black flank feathers are much elongated, but his most extraordinary feature is a set of six very long, wire-like feathers, three behind each eye, which are tipped with paddle-shaped black feather rackets. Females are chestnut-brown on the back, with the head and neck black; there is a white stripe behind the eye, a white moustachial stripe and a black edge to the white throat. The underparts are dark yellowish-brown with narrow dark bars.

Breeding: This has not been described, but in 1973 the first display-arenas of this species were found, 5 m apart in a dense, shrubby area: each was a flat, scrupulously cleared patch and the presence of several small saplings left in the arena followed the pattern of other *Parotia* species. A captive male displayed on the ground, holding his wings high, pretending to peck at the ground, and then stooping abruptly, turning his head right under his breast. Then the tail was thrown up vertically and its outer feathers rapidly opened and closed, fan-like, five or six times. Suddenly the tail was dropped, the body was thrown upright and the long feathers of the back and flanks were raised to form the 'umbrella' seen in other *Parotia* species. The head-plumes were thrown well forward and the brilliant breast-shield was held flat. The bird then turned rapidly from side to side, causing the ends of the long plumes to rotate.

Remarks: This species is hardly known in the wild.

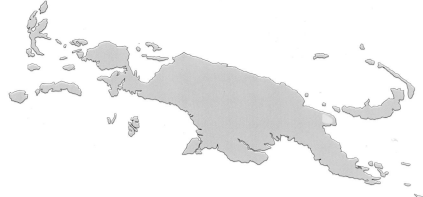

Wahnes' Six-wired Bird of Paradise

Parotia wahnesi

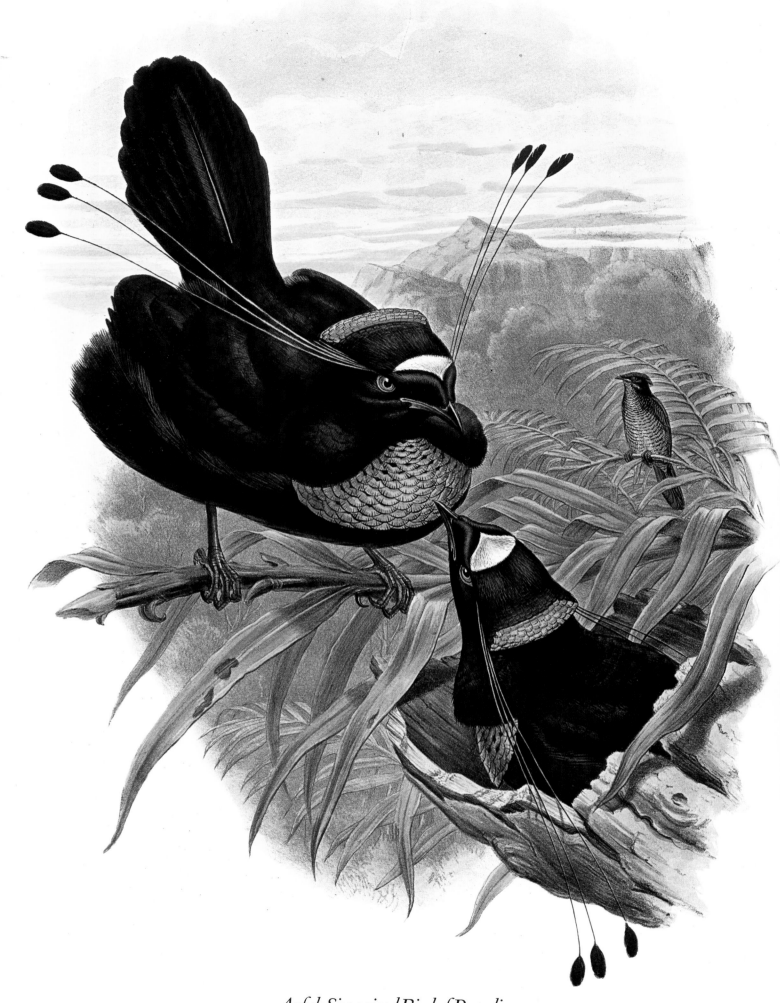

Arfak Six-wired Bird of Paradise

Parotia sefilata

Arfak Six-wired Bird of Paradise
Parotia sefilata

Distribution: New Guinea, confined to the Wandammen Mountains and the mountains of the Vogelkop, from 1200 to 1800 m (*3800 to 5800 ft*).

Description: 305 mm (*12 in*). The male is velvety black above and on the wings and tail, with a white-tipped crest and an iridescent green to violet nape-patch. Behind each eye are three long, erectile wire-like shafts, each with paddle-shaped black rackets at the end. There is an iridescent golden green breast shield and the remainder of the underparts, including the elongated plumes at the sides of the breast, are black. The female has a black head, with a grey line flecked with black running back from the gape, and is brown above, with a greyish throat flecked and barred with blackish-brown and greyish underparts with narrow brownish-black bars.

Breeding: Polygamous. The nest and eggs are unknown, but the display has been described. Each male prepares an arena, roughly 1 to 1.5 m (*3 to 5 ft*) across, in dense undergrowth, keeping it clear of leaves and other debris. He stands on this with his head raised and his bill pointing upwards and, extending his neck, turns the long head-plumes forwards, sideways and downwards, at the same time spreading the flank plumes around his body like a skirt in what is called the 'umbrella pose'; the white feathers of the crest are shown as the head tips forward. Then the head is moved forwards, left and right, so that the racket-ended plumes swing in all directions, while the skirt extends still further and almost encircles the body. The display ends with a brief, stiff-legged dance in a half-circle, the head still swinging to and fro.

Remarks: This is a relatively common species which feeds on various fruits.

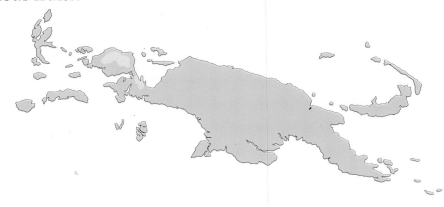

Queen Carola's Six-wired Bird of Paradise

Parotia carolae

Distribution: New Guinea, in the central mountains from Weyland to the Victor Emanuel mountains, between 1200 and 1800 m (*3800 and 6000 ft*).

Description: 240 mm (*9½ in*). Males are black, tinged with bronze on the upperparts, with an erectile white-tipped crest which conceals a second, gold-tipped crest folded into the dish–shaped skull and which, when erected, forms a crest which reaches forward over the bill. From short tufts of fine feathers above the ear-coverts spring six elongated, wire-like shafts, three on each side, each tipped with a black oval racket. The lower throat is whitish and on the upper breast there is a shield of iridescent violet and lilac, tinged with green and gold. The much-elongated flank plumes are partly white and chestnut. Females are brown above, with a greyish, irregular superciliary stripe and a greyish line below the eye, and with dark barring on the yellowish underparts.

Breeding: Polygamous, but the nest, eggs and display are unknown. Presumably displays are similar to those of the Arfak species, with much use of the 'umbrella pose' and movement of the six racket-tipped wires. At any rate, this species maintains an arena rather like that of *P. sefilata*, though a little larger, and like that species has various convenient perches above and around it. The conspicuous presence of red and yellow seeds in droppings on the arena might possibly have some significance.

Remarks: This seems to be a scarce species and certainly its life-history is largely unknown. It feeds on fruit and berries.

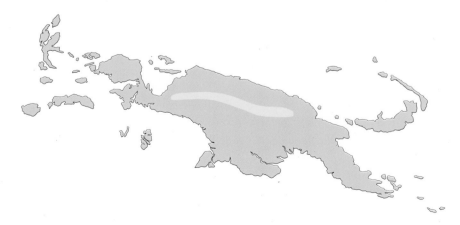

Queen Carola's Six-wired Bird of Paradise

Parotia carolae

Lawes' Six-wired Bird of Paradise

Parotia lawesi

Distribution: New Guinea, in the mountains of the south-east, from 1000 to 1400 m (*3200 to 4500 ft*).

Description: 260 mm (*10¼ in*). As in the other *Parotia* species, the male is largely black, in this case with a glossy purple-blue patch on the nape and a forehead crest which is erectile and white to dark brown, or gold to dark brown in one race. Six elongated wire-like shafts, three on each side, are tipped with black feather-rackets and extend from tufts above the ear-coverts. A broad breast-shield is iridescent bronze-green, tinged with some blue, but otherwise the underparts are all blackish, with the greatly elongated flank plumes common to this genus. Females are reddish brown above, blackish on the head with a greyish moustachial stripe, and deep yellowish-brown, barred darker, on the underparts.

Breeding: Polygamous. The nest is a shallow cup of fine plant stems, lined with small roots, probably placed in the fork of a branch, in which one egg is laid, reddish with dark rufous or blackish patches and spots and some greyish spots. This species maintains a display arena or dance area similar to that of the Arfak bird and its ground display is also very similar. In one display, the male stands erect and raises the very long flank feathers at right-angles to the back and also erects the feathers of the lower breast and abdomen to complete the umbrella pose. Then the bird dances – moving about 60 cm to the right, 60 cm to the left, and back again, with deliberate short hops; during all this the head moves quickly from side to side so that the feather-rackets on the long wires bob about crazily. The climax is reached when the motion of the head increases so that the rackets become a blur.

Remarks: This is a common but rather local species of the upper part of the forest, whose chief foods are fruit and seeds.

Lawes' Six-wired Bird of Paradise

Parotia lawesi

King of Saxony Bird of Paradise
Pteridophora alberti

Distribution: New Guinea, in the central mountains from 1500 to 2600 m (*5000 to 8500 ft*), from the Weyland Mountains to the south-east of the island.

Description: 220 mm (*8¾ in*). The extraordinary-looking male has basically black and yellow plumage – black on the head and upper breast and on the entire upperparts, with a bronze tinge on the back, orange-buff wing-patches and yellowish underparts. There is a narrow fringe of iridescent violet-blue feathers on the upper breast and the feathers of the upper back are elongated to form a distinct cape. But his most incredible adornments are two immensely long (up to 400 mm/*16 in*) white, wire-like shafts protruding from behind the eyes; on the outer edge of each shaft there are up to 44 horny scallops, glossy pale blue in colour. In contrast, the female is brownish-grey above, greyer on the head and neck and darker on the lower back, often with a spike-like grey feather extending from behind the eye. Her underparts are whitish, boldly barred with black on the breast and flanks.

Breeding: Polygamous. The nest and eggs remain undescribed, but males are known to have favourite display perches high in forest trees (25 to 29 m/*80 to 90 ft* up), spaced roughly 360 m (*400 yd*) from one another. They call often – a long, hissing note ending in a sharp rasp, audible over long distances. In display, the male raises the long head plumes steeply above his back and moves his body so violently that his perch moves up and down vigorously – and all the while the black cape opens and closes. Slowly, the head is brought forward and downward, bringing the long plumes forward – about twelve times in every fifty bounces on the perch. Throughout, he makes a hissing noise.

Remarks: This is a species of middle and upper mountain cloud forests and feeds on fruits.

King of Saxony Bird of Paradise

Pteridophora alberti

King Bird of Paradise

Cicinnurus regius

King Bird of Paradise
Cicinnurus regius

Distribution: New Guinea, throughout, from sea-level to 800 m (*2500 ft*). Also the Aru Islands, Misol, Salawati and Batanta in the Western Papuan Islands and Japen Island (Geelvink Bay).

Description: 125–165 mm (*5–6½ in*). The very handsome male is glossy crimson on the head, neck and upperparts, more orange on the forehead and tail, with a glossy black-green patch over the eye. The two central tail-feathers are elongated into wire-like shafts tipped with emerald green rackets. At the upper breast the deep, purplish-crimson feathers are edged with buff, with a glossy green breast-band below, and at the sides of the breast there is an ashy, erectile fan, with bands of grey and brown towards its end and emerald-green tips. The rest of the underparts are white. Females are brown above, more olive on the head and darker on the wings and wing-coverts, which are also edged with chestnut; the buffish underparts are barred with brown.

Breeding: Polygamous. The nest is made in a natural hole in a tree in which two eggs are laid, creamy with brown streaks at the larger end. Each male has his own display area, fairly high in a densely-foliaged tree. Several displays have been described, including one in which he raises his tail-wires aloft, spreads his wings and then hangs upside-down from his perch with his wings spread and vibrating and his beak open to show off his yellow-green mouth. More typically, a male sings a warbling song to a female, expanding his breast fan and puffing up his white underpart feathers so that he becomes almost spherical. His tail-shafts are raised with the rackets above his head and the head itself is raised and swayed from side to side.

Remarks: A fairly common bird in lowland forests, their species is hard to see but often heard calling. It feeds on tree fruits.

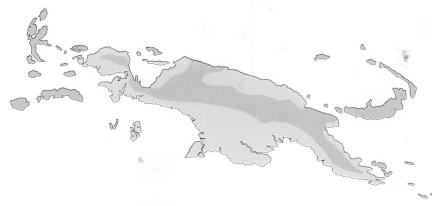

Magnificent Bird of Paradise
Diphyllodes magnificus

Distribution: New Guinea – throughout the island from 600 to 1500 m (*1900 to 5000 ft*) and also on Misol, Salawati and Japen Islands.

Description: 198 mm (*7¾ in*). The male is brown on the crown and nape, with a short fan of glossy pale yellow behind, and a glossy deep red back with a narrow black band above the orange lower back and rump. On the wings, the greater coverts and secondaries are glossy orange yellow, while the black tail has the central feathers elongated into two very narrow, curled streamers. There is a tuft of brown feathers at the side of the neck and the breast-shield is deep glossy green with a central band of iridescent blue-green. The female is olive-brown above, darker on the head and wings, and grey-buff below with fine black barring.

Breeding: Polygamous. The nest is built at no great height in a small tree or bush and is made of mosses, leaves, small roots, plant fibres and the like. Two eggs are laid, creamy yellow with brown and grey markings. Each male maintains a display arena, a thoroughly cleared area 4.5 to 6 m (*15 to 20 ft*) across, in which denuded saplings are left – it is on these vertical saplings that he displays, spreading his breast-shield and the yellow, cape-like fan on his hindneck and, when a female is present, opening his bill wide to expose its yellow-green interior.

Remarks: This is a common species, more easily heard than seen, and one whose spiralling tail-feathers are often worn by natives. It feeds largely on tree fruits.

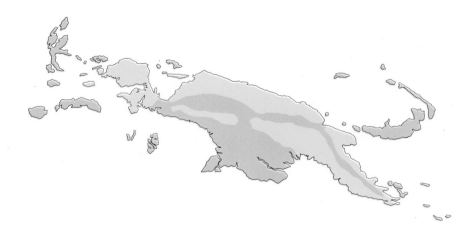

Magnificent Bird of Paradise

Diphyllodes magnificus

Wilson's Bird of Paradise

Diphyllodes respublica

Distribution: New Guinea, confined to the hilly interior of Waigeu and Batanta in the Western Papuan Islands.

Description: 165 mm (*6½ in*). The male has a naked blue crown and a short fan of pale yellow on his black nape. The glossy red back has black sides and the rump is blackish with a red wash; the wings are black with red on the inner secondaries and the black tail has its two central feathers elongated into fine, curved projections. Below the black head and neck there is a breast-shield of glossy green, with a few iridescent blue spots, and the remaining underparts are brownish with a purple gloss. Females lack the ornamental plumes and are generally brown above and buffish below, with narrow brownish bars on the underparts.

Breeding: Polygamous. The nest and eggs have not been described, but the cleared display area is much like that of the closely related Magnificent Bird of Paradise, *D. magnificus*. Partial displays have been described involving captive birds, which included calling with low whistling notes, jerking the head and opening the bill to show the vivid green gape and raising and spreading the breast-shield.

Remarks: Although this is apparently a common bird on Waigeu and Batanta, very little is known of its life history. It is named after the English ornithologist Edward Wilson.

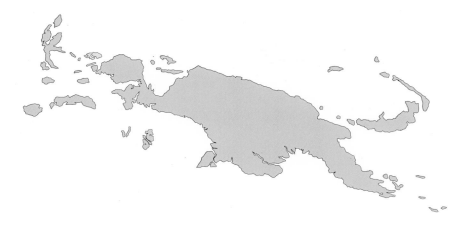

Wilson's Bird of Paradise

Diphyllodes respublica

Greater Bird of Paradise
Paradisaea apoda

Distribution: New Guinea – the southern part, mostly west of the Fly River, and also on the Aru Islands. Lowlands, up to 900 m (*3000 ft*). Successfully introduced and still surviving in small numbers on Little Tobago in the Caribbean.

Description: 430–460 mm (*17–18 in*). The male is a spectacular bird, with a glossy green-black face and throat, an orange-yellow crown and hindneck, maroon-brown upperparts, wings and tail and mainly maroon-brown underparts. Its most striking feature is a great train of fine plumes springing from the sides of the breast, yellow to orange (with a few maroon feathers) for the most part, then cinnamon on their outer ends. The two central tail-feathers extend into dark, wire-like plumes. The female is mainly maroon-brown, darker on the head and neck and paler on the breast and abdomen, lacking the ornamental plumes.

Breeding: Polygamous. The nest has not been described, but the two eggs are brownish-buff with reddish and blackish streaks. Groups of males gather in the treetops and display communally, with a sort of hierarchy from the most magnificently plumed male downwards; their wings are held out like oars, the back is arched and the tail is depressed under the perch. Gradually, with much shaking, the long flank-plumes are expanded and spread until they extend straight upwards, forming a colourful cascade which almost conceals the rest of the bird. Jumps and charges follow about the display area, often involving several males, to the accompaniment of harsh calling. When a female appears, a male retires to his own personal display place and freezes in a display pose with the flank plumes fully expanded.

Remarks: This was one of the first birds of paradise to be seen in Europe, where its skins were often shown minus the feet – hence the name *apoda*, 'footless'. It is active, noisy and gregarious.

Greater Bird of Paradise

Paradisaea apoda

Count Raggi's Bird of Paradise

Paradisaea raggiana

Count Raggi's Bird of Paradise
Paradisaea raggiana

Distribution: New Guinea, in the south-central and eastern parts, in lowlands to 1700 m (*5700 ft*).

Description: 330–355 mm (*13–14 in*). The male has a black, green glossed face and throat, a pale yellow crown and nape and largely maroon upperparts, wings and tail – but with yellow on the rump in some races and a yellow bar on the middle wing-coverts. There is a yellow band across the throat, joining the yellow on the nape (but this is absent in one race) above a purplish-black breast; the remaining underparts are maroon. Enormous ornamental plumes spring from the sides of the breast, forming a huge train, mainly red but growing paler and edged with grey and cinnamon towards their tips. Two very long tail-wires are blackish in colour. Females are largely maroon and lack the ornamental plumes; the crown and nape are washed with pale yellow.

Breeding: Polygamous. A basin-shaped nest of vines and leaves is built, in which a single egg is laid, pinkish-cream with red-brown streaks and spots. Males gather in small groups in the treetops, but 5 to 30 m (*20 to 100 ft*) apart, each on his own display branch. In display, the head is lowered and the raised wings are brought together with an audible thump. The great spray of flank-plumes is expanded upwards and backwards and the bird's body vibrates visibly. When females approach, males prance about their display perches, very acrobatically, and may even hang upside-down while still retaining the full display posture.

Remarks: This is another common, noisy and conspicuous species and is one which does not appear to have suffered at the hand of man, either through plume-hunting or the advance of agriculture.

Lesser Bird of Paradise

Paradisaea minor

Distribution: New Guinea – northern and western parts of the island, also Japen Island (Geelvink Bay) and Misol Island (Western Papuan Islands). Sea level to 1700 m (*5700 ft*).

Description: 330 mm (*13 in*). This is the third species in which the male is basically maroon-brown, but with a black, green glossed face, a yellow crown and nape and a yellow back. There is a narrow yellow bar on the wing coverts, the central tail-feathers are elongated into two dark 'wires' and there is an enormous train of fine plumes at either side of the breast – golden-yellow but white tinged with lavender towards the tips. The female is dull maroon above, with a brown head and a yellow wash on the hind neck and white underparts.

Breeding: Polygamous. The nest is cup-shaped, built of vines and sticks, at no great height in a fork of a branch, and in it one egg is laid, creamy with streaks and patches of brown and purplish-grey. Males gather in groups in traditional treetop display areas and their full display consists of lowering the head, extending the wings outwards and raising the flank plumes so that they cascade over the back. There is a good deal of dancing and chasing and periods of loud calling. Males 'freeze' in display posture when performing to females.

Remarks: This is a common species, eating both fruit and insects, and is often found near human habitations.

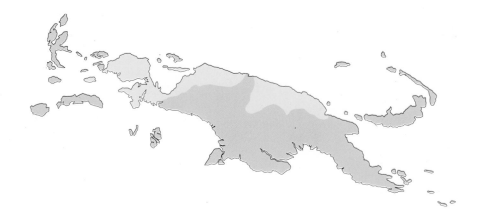

Lesser Bird of Paradise

Paradisaea minor

Goldie's Bird of Paradise
Paradisaea decora

Distribution: New Guinea, confined to the D'Entrecasteaux Archipelago. In mountains, usually over 500 m (*1500 ft*).

Description: 305–330 mm (*12–13 in*). The very distinctive male is more or less glossy yellow above, washed with orange, especially on the head. The face is black, glossed green, and the throat metallic green above an obscure yellow collar; the remaining underparts are lavender-grey and on each side of the breast is a huge erectile train of fine, deep crimson plumes, becoming browner towards their tips. At the base of each spray of plumes is a large tuft of red and grey, tipped with purplish-black. The two central tail-feathers are elongated into blackish 'wires'. The female is mainly dull olive above, washed with yellow, with a yellow head and a brownish-black throat. Her underparts are dull buffish indistinctly barred with brown.

Breeding: Presumably polygamous, as in other *Paradisaea* species. Their display is possibly like that of *P. raggiana*.

Remarks: This species is almost unknown in the wild. It is believed to be a much less advanced *Paradisaea* than the previous three species, having evolved much more slowly in the isolation of the islands where it lives.

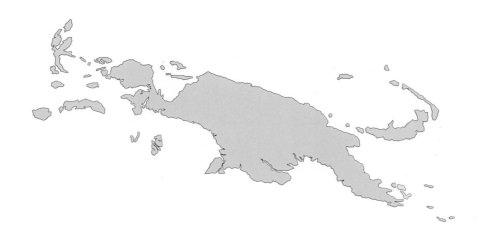

Goldie's Bird of Paradise

Paradisaea decora

Red Bird of Paradise

Paradisaea rubra

Distribution: New Guinea, confined to the Western Papuan Islands of Waigen, Batanta and Saonet, and possibly Ghemien.

Description: 330 mm (*13 in*). The face and throat of the male are iridescent green, with prominent feather pompoms over each eye; otherwise the upperparts, upper wing-coverts and sides of the breast are orange-yellow, with the centre of the back bright rufous, the rump yellow and the wings and tail reddish-brown. The underparts are maroon-brown, but at each side of the breast there is a very large train of ornamental plumes, mostly glossy crimson with greyish tips. The central tail-feathers are elongated and twisted. Females resemble males, but lack the long plumes and are browner on the head and yellower on the body.

Breeding: Polygamous, but the nest and eggs have not been described so far. The fullest display descriptions come from studies of captive birds which show that this species uses vertical perches, climbing and swinging into upside-down positions, with much bill-clicking, swaying and opening and shivering of the wings. Unlike similar *Paradisaea* species, this one scarcely displays its flank plumes at all and more emphasis seems to be placed on showing off the head plumage. Displays are certainly very complex and are not a simplified form of *Paradisaea*-type display as was originally thought: the dance sequences on a vertical perch resemble those of the *Diphyllodes* and *Cicinnurus* birds of paradise and seem to establish a much closer link between these genera and *Paradisaea* than with other birds of paradise.

Remarks: Although this is a common and conspicuously noisy bird, it is very little known in the wild.

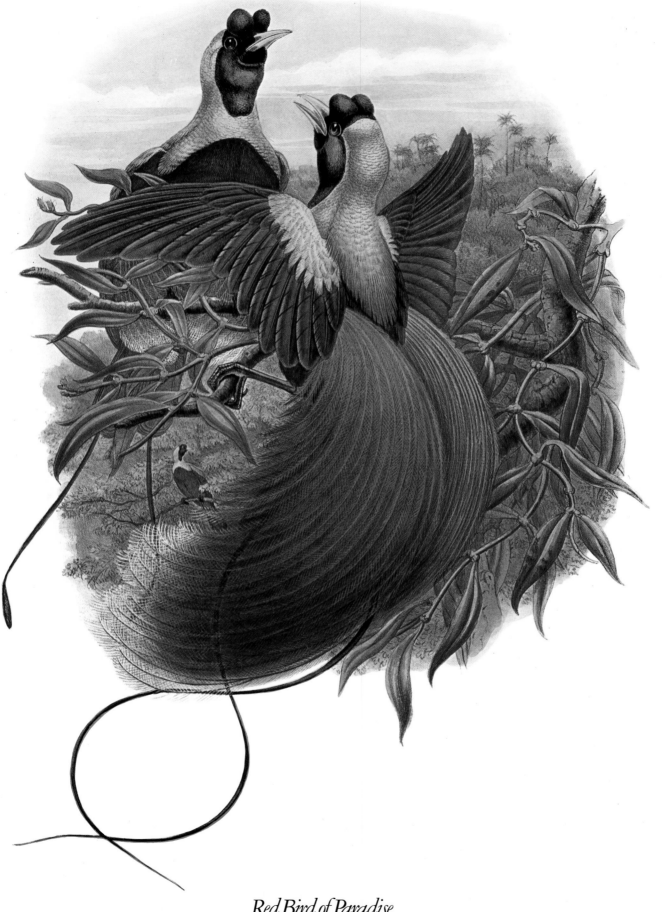

Red Bird of Paradise

Paradisaea rubra

Emperor of Germany Bird of Paradise
Paradisaea guilielmi

Distribution: New Guinea, restricted to the Huon Peninsula, from around 700 to 1700 m (*2200 to 5500 ft*) and rarely to 1800 m (*6000 ft*).

Description: 320–330 mm (*12½–13 in*). Males have iridescent green crowns, faces and throats, and are otherwise wholly yellow above, apart from deep maroon on the lower back. There is an incomplete yellow collar above the dark maroon underparts and immense ornamental sprays of feathers grow out from the sides of the breast, mainly ivory-coloured and yellower towards the base. As in the other *Paradisaea* species, the central tail-feathers extend into two very long, wire-like projections. Females resemble males, without the ornamental plumes, but are browner on the head and have rather paler underparts, sometimes with dark barring.

Breeding: Polygamous. The nest has not been described, but one or two eggs are laid, creamy to cinnamon and streaked with grey and reddish-brown. Little is known of the display organization of wild birds, though they are believed to display in groups, but captive birds have been observed in some detail. The male bobs up and down, spreading and vibrating his wings and raising and spreading his flank-plumes. Suddenly the bird calls and turns head-first under the perch, with the wings held outwards and the spread tail pointing upwards; then the flank-plumes spread to form a great mass of feathers around the lower body, with the head, wings and tail outside. The body sways from side to side so that the ornamental plumes sway this way and that; the whole display may last for 5 minutes.

Remarks: This too is a common species, but little is known of its habits in the wild.

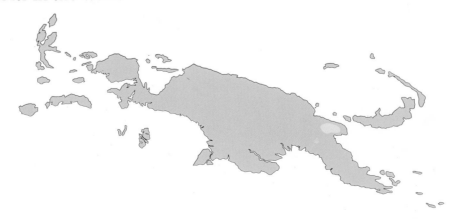

Emperor of Germany Bird of Paradise

Paradisaea guilielmi

Blue Bird of Paradise
Paradisaea rudolphi

Distribution: New Guinea, in the mountain forests of the eastern part, from 1400 to 1900 m (*4500 to 6300 ft*).

Description: 290 mm (*11¼ in*). The beautiful male is largely black, with maroon on the crown and nape, white spots above and below the eye, grey-blue on the lower back, a bronze tinge on the throat and an indistinct cobalt-blue breast-band; his wings, apart from some brown on the outer secondaries and the largely black primaries, are blue, as is the tail. At each side of the breast there is a short tuft of rusty-red feathers, followed by a much elongated spray of ornamental plumes, first cobalt, then opalescent blue and then, on their outer third, pale purplish-blue. The two central tail-feathers are greatly elongated and wire-like, often with a small blue spot near the tip. Females lack the ornamental plumes but otherwise resemble males, except that their breasts are deep maroon to reddish-brown and the remaining underparts are reddish-brown.

Breeding: Polygamous. A basin-shaped nest is built in a low tree fork, in which a single egg is laid, creamy with reddish-brown and grey streaks. In display, males hang upside-down from a branch, with the ornamental plumes spread into the shape of an inverted triangle and the long central tail-feathers held upright but drooping down to either side from about halfway along their length. The body moves back and forth and these movements have the effect of spreading the plumes fully and producing marvellous changing colour effects. The male also sings softly in display – a feature not noted in other birds of paradise.

Remarks: This species is common in parts of its range, but again its habits have been little studied in the wild. Like the other *Paradisaea* species, it is largely a fruit eater.

Blue Bird of Paradise

Paradisaea rudolphi

White-eared Catbird

Ailuroedus buccoides

Distribution: New Guinea and the Western Papuan Islands, from sea level to 900 m (*3000 ft*).

Description: 250 mm (*10 in*). The sexes are alike, but for the female's slightly smaller size and her paler crown feathers. The crown varies from dark to mustard brown and the pale brown neck–feathers have black tips, so that a prominent collar is formed above the emerald upperparts. There are small white spots at the tips of the inner secondaries. The area from behind the eye onto the throat is whitish, while the underparts are buffish to chestnut with a variable amount of bold black spotting.

Breeding: Monogamous. A cup-shaped nest is built, at no great height in a small tree, in which a cream-coloured egg is laid. The display of this species has not been described in full, though males are believed to defend territories in which they have been seen displaying to intruder males by bowing and stretching the head and neck downwards, calling with a low, rasping note, and by attacking and chasing them away.

Remarks: This species, which feeds on tree fruits and berries, is common in lowland forest areas – but while its rasping calls are often heard it remains a difficult bird to observe and not much is known of its habits in the wild.

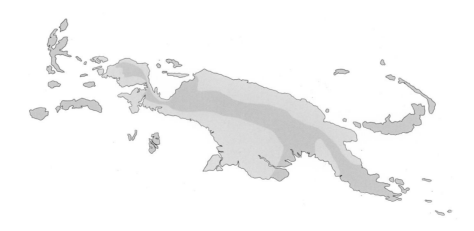

White-eared Catbird

Ailuroedus buccoides

Green Catbird

Ailuroedus crassirostris

Distribution: South-eastern and eastern Australia, from the Shoalham River, New South Wales, north to the Bunya Mountains of southern Queensland.

Description: 305–330 mm (*12–13 in*). The sexes are alike, but with the female slightly smaller. The upperparts are olive-green, with white freckling on the nape, the face mottled with black and green and white tips to the inner wing-feathers, while the underparts are largely pale green, spotted with greenish-white, greyer on the throat and buffish-yellow on the belly. The large, fairly stout bill is pinkish-white.

Breeding: Monogamous. An open, cup-shaped nest is built of vines and twigs, interwoven with leaves and fibres, usually at no great height in vines or in a low tree, in which two creamy-white eggs are laid. Males appear to defend a territory and have been observed courtship-chasing females, all the while emitting their curious cat-like calls (also said to be uncannily like a crying baby). The laying of leaves at prescribed places, suggesting some form of bower behaviour, has recently been observed in this species.

Remarks: This species is not very well known, but it is fairly common and feeds on fruits and berries in rain-forest country. Small flocks are seen outside the breeding season. It has been regarded as a subspecies of the Spotted Catbird by some authorities, but although undoubtedly closely related is now generally given specific status.

Green Catbird

Ailuroedus crassirostris

Spotted or Black-eared Catbird

Ailuroedus melanotis

Distribution: New Guinea, widespread on the main island but also on the Aru and Western Papuan Islands; also Australia, in the Cairns district of northern Queensland. Sometimes at or near sea-level, but mainly from 900 to 1700 m (*3000 to 5600 ft*).

Description: 280–305 mm (*11–12 in*). The sexes are alike, and this species resembles the Green Catbird, *A. crassirostris*, except that the head and chin are black, spotted with grey-brown, and the ear-coverts are noticeably dark brown or black. The feathers of the upper back are grey to reddish-brown, with dark margins giving a noticeably scalloped appearance. Some variation in these markings is seen in the nine subspecies currently recognized.

Breeding: Monogamous. The nest is rather large and bulky, loosely built of sticks with a cup of dead leaves lined with thin plant stems, in which two light olive-brown eggs are laid. Displays do not appear to have been described, but presumably they resemble those known for the Green Catbird.

Remarks: This is a common and widespread species, living in rain forest where it feeds on fruits and seeds, and is sometimes found in small flocks outside the breeding season. Nevertheless, it is a wary bird and is rather difficult to observe. It shares the cat-like yowling notes of the other *Ailuroedus* species and also has a hissing alarm-note.

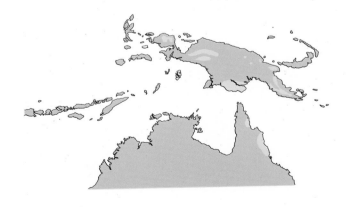

Spotted or Black-eared Catbird

Ailuroedus melanotis

Tooth-billed Catbird

Ailuroedus dentirostris

Tooth-billed Catbird

Ailuroedus dentirostris

Distribution: Australia, from the Cairns district of northern Queensland south to the Seaview Range and the Herbert River region; 600 to 1200 m (*2000 to 4000 ft*), but only rarely in lowlands.

Description: 265 mm (*10½ in*). The sexes are alike – adults are dark olive-brown above, with a whitish or buffish patch at the side of the lower throat, and the underparts buffish-white broadly streaked with dark greyish-brown. The short, stout bill has a strongly curved upper mandible with a distinct notch or tooth near its tip.

Breeding: Polygamous. A saucer-shaped nest of twigs is built in thick foliage, well above the ground, in which two creamy-brown eggs are laid. Each male forms a rudimentary bower or stage – a meticulously cleared area which he decorates with fresh green leaves, placed upside-down and brought in daily; these are secured using his specially modified bill. As many as a hundred leaves may decorate the bower. The male displays on the 'stage', singing loudly and musically (mimicking many other birds) on a special perch close to the stage itself.

Remarks: Until recently, this species was given its own generic name, *Scenopoeetes*, but it is now regarded as a member of the genus *Ailuroedus*. Nevertheless, it shows a number of interesting differences from the other catbirds – it is polygamous and builds a simple bower, while they are monogamous and are not bower-builders (with the possible exception of *A. crassirostris*). Only the male uses its modified bill structure in a special way. Also called the Tooth-billed or Stagemaker Bowerbird.

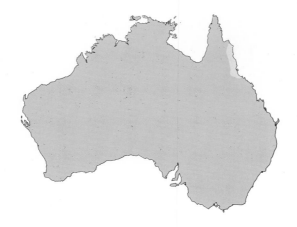

Archbold's Bowerbird

Archboldia papuensis

Archbold's Bowerbird

Archboldia papuensis

Distribution: New Guinea, confined to two distinct and separate areas – Mt Hagen and Mt Giluwe in the east and the Snow Mountains in the west, from Lake Habbema west to the Weyland Mountains. 2000 to 3700 m (*6700 to 12,000 ft*).

Description: 370 mm (*14½ in*). Males of the western population are dark sooty-grey, with olive on the outer flight-feathers and traces of yellow on the crown (though full adults may not have been found yet), while eastern birds are jet-black with a prominent golden-yellow crest. Females are greyer with a pale yellowish patch on the leading edge of the wing.

Breeding: Polygamous. The nest and eggs have yet to be described. The male makes and tends a bower, about 1.6 m (*5 ft*) wide, comprising a mat of fern fronds, decorated at the edges with black beetle wing-cases, blue-black and grey snail shells, blue berries and black and amber resin chips from tree ferns. Some fern fronds are draped on branches around and above the bower and on nearby fallen tree trunks and horizontal branches the bird places green fruits, bits of charcoal and whitish snail shells. Males attract females to their bowers by calling and displaying to them with a crawling motion across the floor of the bower, churring and holding their fluttering wings and tail partly opened.

Remarks: This bird was discovered as recently as 1939, in the west of its range, and was named for Richard Archbold, a noted New Guinea ornithological explorer. The eastern population was found in 1950. So far, only the bowers of the eastern birds are known and it is uncertain whether males in the west were fully mature when described – several apparent differences between the two populations remain to be investigated before it can be finally established whether there are two similar species, or two separated races of one species (as is believed at present).

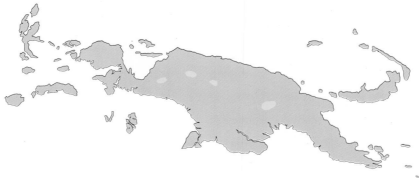

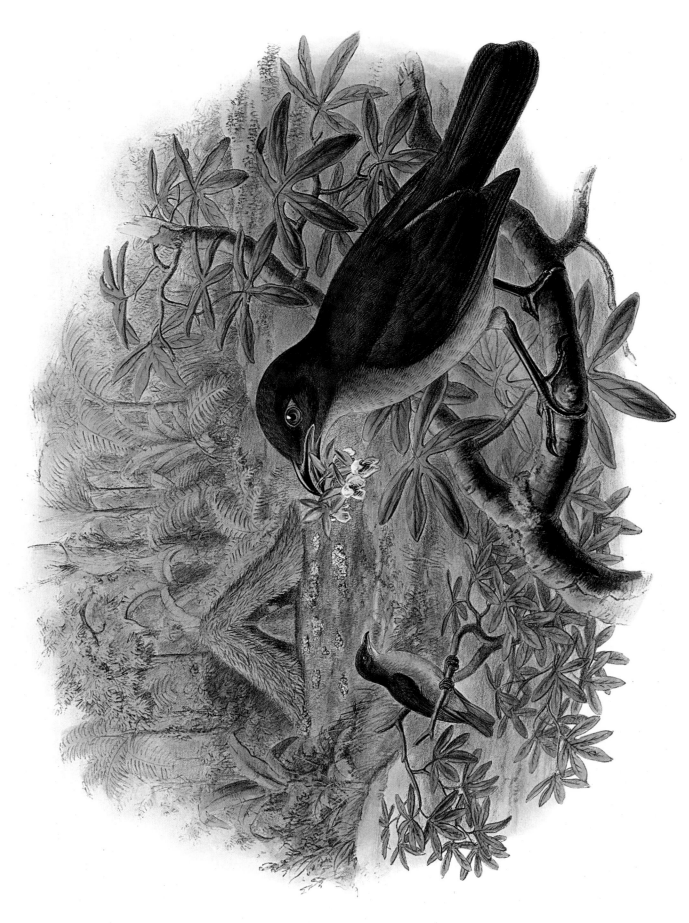

Vogelkop Gardener Bowerbird

Amblyornis inornatus

Vogelkop Gardener Bowerbird

Amblyornis inornatus

Distribution: New Guinea. Confined to the mountains of the Vogelkop and the adjoining Wandammen Mountains, from 1200 to 1800 m (*3800 to 5800 ft*).

Description: 250 mm (*10 in*). The adults are alike, with the female slightly smaller, being largely dark olive-brown above, with a light amber tinge on the upper back, a darker crown and pale buffish or yellowish underparts.

Breeding: Polygamous. The nest and eggs are unknown, but the extraordinary bower is well documented. This is a cone-shaped 'hut', made of twigs piled round a sapling to a height of about three feet, open on one side to form a wide door. Inside the hut the floor is kept meticulously clear of all débris, and on a small cleared 'lawn' in front of the door the male places small piles of yellow or blue fruit, bits of charcoal, small black stones, big mushrooms and freshly-picked flowers. Even red shotgun cartridge cases have been used as decoration. Observations on the actual display are very limited, but in one case on record the male entered his bower to the accompaniment of a wide range of excited calls (including some mimicked from other birds), crouching and scurrying around excitedly inside.

Remarks: This is a common bird within its limited range and is particularly well known among the natives as a marvellous mimic of other species.

Macgregor's Gardener Bowerbird
Amblyornis macgregoriae

Distribution: New Guinea, in the mountain forests of the main body of the island and in the Huon and south-eastern peninsulas, from 1200 to 2700 m (*3800 to 9000 ft*).

Description: 265 mm (*10½ in*). The male is basically olive-brown above, with an amber tint to the feathers of the head, and clay-brown below, with some white streaks on the upper breast, a yellowish wash on the abdomen, pale orange-yellow inner edges to the flight feathers and orange-yellow on the under-wings. His most striking feature is a large golden-orange crest, edged and tipped with brown. The female is like the male, but lacks the crest.

Breeding: Polygamous. The nest is a deep cup of bark, small roots and leaves, in a small forest tree, in which a single yellow-ish-white egg is laid. Each male seems to have his own bower, a saucer of moss perhaps 1 m (*3 ft*) across and up to 15 cm (*6 in*) deep, sometimes with pieces of whitish or black lichen at its rim or just outside it, with a central column built of twigs and sticks up to 41 cm (*16 in*) in length, criss-crossed around a supporting sapling stem to a height of 1 or 1.2 m (*3 or 4 ft*). Berries and insect silk may be used to decorate the column. The male is never far from his bower, to which he appears to attract females by constant calling; his display has not been described in full, but is known to involve the use of his spectacular crest.

Remarks: This is a common but wary bird of the upper mountain forests, where it feeds on tree fruits. Its crest feathers are much prized for decoration by natives.

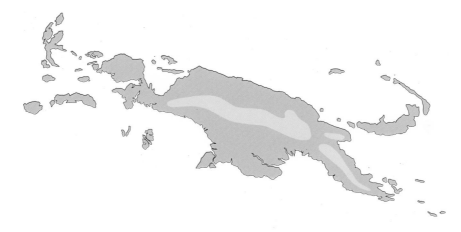

Macgregor's Gardener Bowerbird

Amblyornis macgregoriae

Striped Gardener Bowerbird

Amblyornis subalaris

Striped Gardener Bowerbird

Amblyornis subalaris

Distribution: New Guinea, in the mountains of the south-east from 700 to 1100 m (*2200 to 3600 ft*).

Description: 223 mm (*8¾ in*). The male has the head and whole upperparts dark olive-brown, darker on the forehead, and a broad erectile crest, variable in size and colour but generally glossy golden-orange tipped and edged with dark brown. The underparts are olive-brown with pale yellowish streaks, especially on the breast and abdomen. Females closely resemble males but lack the crest and are rather paler.

Breeding: Polygamous. A cup-shaped nest is built in which at least one egg is laid, yellowish-white in colour. Nothing is known of this species' courtship behaviour, but the male builds an untidy hut-like structure of twigs, about 60 cm (*2 ft*) high, about a supporting sapling, with a wide open door at the front. An arena of open ground is maintained in front of this door, and this is covered with black fibres from tree ferns; on this are placed flowers, berries, brightly coloured leaves and beetles' wing-cases.

Remarks: Though apparently not uncommon, this remains a little-known bowerbird and one which has proved very difficult to watch in the wild. It replaces Macgregor's Bowerbird at lower altitudes. The splendid crest-feathers are much sought after by natives.

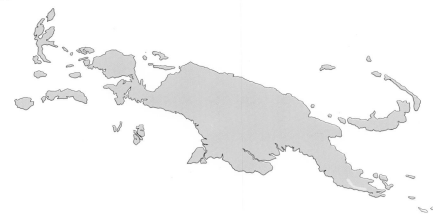

Yellow-fronted Gardener Bowerbird
Amblyornis flavifrons

Distribution: Unknown, but possibly confined to the western mountain forests of New Guinea and/or the Western Papuan Islands.

Description: 240 mm (*9½ in*). The female is unknown, but the male has dark reddish-brown upperparts, an olive-brown head with a broad, bright yellow crown and crest and buffish-yellow underparts.

Breeding: Totally unknown.

Remarks: Nothing is known of this bird, except for what can be learned from only four known museum skins, all of males, which appeared in Europe during the heyday of the plumage trade in the early years of this century. It has never been found in the wild, in spite of at least a dozen attempts to locate it, and among bower-birds and birds of paradise is unique in this respect. It may be either a very rare bird or one which is virtually extinct – but it is almost certainly one which has a very restricted range. The disposition of the primary wing feathers of this species differs considerably from others in the genus. The shape of the wing and the narrow feathers may indicate a much more open habitat than thick forest.

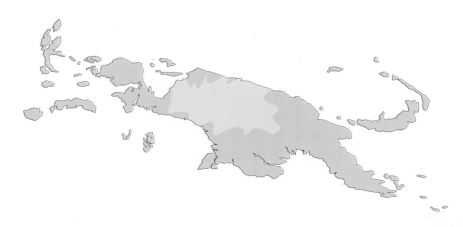

Yellow-fronted Gardener Bowerbird

Amblyornis flavifrons

Golden Bowerbird

Prionodura newtoniana

Distribution: Australia, confined to the mountain forests, mainly from 900 to 1600 m (*3000 to 5400 ft*), in the Atherton-Cairns district of northern Queensland.

Description: 230–240 mm (*9–9½ in*). The male has the centre of the crown, the nape, the sides of the tail and the underparts bright orange-yellow; elsewhere he is dull golden-brown, with a noticeable sheen on the feathers of the upperparts and throat. The very different female is basically dark olive-brown above and ash-grey below.

Breeding: Polygamous. The nest is a shallow cup of twigs, leaves and mosses, in tangled undergrowth near the ground, in which two white or creamy eggs are laid. Groups of bowers occur fairly close together, each being maintained by a single male. A bower is built around two saplings or small trees: around each, sticks are piled into pyramids, one pile usually rather higher than the other and as much as 2 or 2.5 m (*7 or 8 ft*) high. Sticks are 'glued' together (as they are in the nest of this species) by a slimy fungus. A stick or vine in the cleared area between the pyramids is intermeshed with them, forming a bridged 'maypole' around which the display takes place. The bower may be decorated with moss, lichens, ferns, flowers and berries. Often, a series of small ancillary pyramids of sticks is found within the bower area and the size, shape and layout is very variable around the basic pattern of two pyramids with their connecting arch.

Remarks: This species is quite common and withstood extensive collecting of both eggs and specimens following its discovery late in the 19th century. It feeds mainly on fruits and berries, but also takes some insects.

Golden Bowerbird

Prionodura newtoniana

Golden Regent Bowerbird
Sericulus aureus

Distribution: New Guinea, in the foothills and lower mountains of the main island, including the Vogelkop, from sea-level to 1400 m (*4500 ft*).

Description: 250 mm (*10 in*). The male has a golden-red crown, crest and elongated back-plumes, and is otherwise yellow apart from a black tail with a yellowish tip. Birds from the southern half of the island have a crimson streak around the eye and a yellow throat. Females lack the crest and back plumes and are more or less olive brown on the head and upperparts, pale on the throat and yellow below.

Breeding: The details are virtually unknown and no nest has ever been found. The bower is of the 'avenue' type – two more or less parallel walls of sticks, some almost meeting in an arch over the top, with an avenue between and each entrance built up with sticks. Decorations include purple and white flowers, blue and brown berries, red nuts, black mushrooms and snail shells. The display itself is unknown.

Remarks: This remains one of the least-known bowerbirds and exactly how the bower is used is a matter of debate. It is a shy bird, not easily observed. Some authorities suggest that the distinct southern form may actually be a separate species.

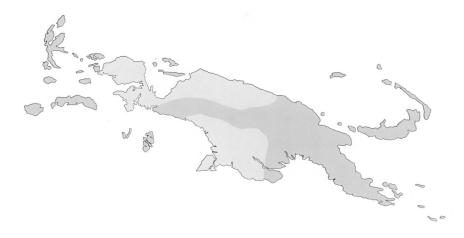

Golden Regent Bowerbird

Sericulus aureus

Adelbert Regent Bowerbird
Sericulus bakeri

Distribution: New Guinea, known only from the Adelbert Mountains, from 900 to 1200 m (*3000 to 4000 ft*).

Description: 273 mm (*10¾ in*). The male is black, with a bluish gloss on the throat and breast, but with a scarlet crown grading to a more orange colour on the nape, an erectile cape of orange-red feathers on the upper back and a yellow wing-patch. The female is dark brown on the head and upperparts, with whitish underparts with a faint yellow wash and much dark barring.

Breeding: Nothing is known of this bird's breeding habits or its bower – if indeed it makes one: opinion is divided on this point, but it does seem likely that a bower is built and if so it presumably resembles those of other *Sericulus* species.

Remarks: Although apparently fairly common within its limited range, this bird is not at all well known. It is noisy and sometimes gregarious, living in the treetops, and is known to feed on various species of insects as well as tree fruits. Although the male was described and the species named fifty years ago, the female was not collected and examined until 1959.

Adelbert Regent Bowerbird

Sericulus bakeri

Australian Regent Bowerbird
Sericulus chrysocephalus

Distribution: Eastern Australia, from New South Wales north to southern Queensland, in coastal and lowland rain forest.

Description: 240–250 mm (*9½–10 in*). The male is an all-black bird, with a bright orange-yellow crown, nape and upper back and broad orange-yellow wing-patches, but the female is very different – rusty-brown on the face and hind neck, with black on the crown, the nape and the centre of the throat, and the back and upper breast blackish-brown spotted with off-white. Her lower breast and belly are whitish with dark brown scallop markings and her wings and tail are brown.

Breeding: Probably polygamous. A saucer-shaped nest of loose twigs is built in tangled vegetation and in this two eggs are laid, whitish or greyish-yellow spotted and finely marked with reddish-brown and purplish-black. Bowers are inconspicuous and not often found, but they are not uncommon or rudimentary, as a number of authors have suggested. A platform of sticks is built, which may be up to 36 cm (*14 in*) long and 25 cm (*10 in*) across, with two side walls of upright sticks, up to 30 cm (*12 in*) high, and the entrances up to 10 cm (*4 in*) across. Various berries, snail shells, leaves, pebbles and even rat-droppings are used for decoration. However, the male's most extraordinary achievement is that he actually paints his bower: holding a small leaf or piece of vegetation in the bill, he mashes this down and applies the resulting pulp, mixed with saliva, to the bower walls with a pecking action – leaving distinct yellowish 'paint-marks'.

Remarks: This is a fairly common but rather shy bird, found mainly in lowland rain forest but sometimes venturing into open orchards and gardens. It feeds on fruits and is also insectivorous.

Australian Regent Bowerbird

Sericulus chrysocephalus

Satin Bowerbind

Ptilonorhynchus violaceus

Satin Bowerbird

Ptilonorhynchus violaceus

Distribution: Eastern Australia, from the Cairns district of northern Queensland south to the Otway Peninsula in Victoria, from sea level to 900 m (*3000 ft*).

Description: 280–290 mm (*11–11½ in*). The male is wholly black, with a deep violet gloss. The very different female is mainly olive-green, darker above and paler below, tinged with yellow on the belly and dark brown scalloping on the underparts.

Breeding: Polygamous. The nest is a shallow saucer of twigs, lined with leaves, usually placed in a tree at no great height above the ground. One to three eggs are laid, creamy or buffish, blotched and streaked with dark brown and grey. Groups of males build bowers in a selected area, each bird maintaining his own private one: the complete bower is a mat or platform of firmly-woven twigs and sticks with side walls of sticks about 30 cm (*1 ft*) high and usually meeting above the platform in an arch. Large amounts of decorative material are used, especially blue-coloured objects, and a fully operational bower is a very colourful sight. Items used include many flowers, berries, fruits, parrot feathers, fungi, snail shells and even snakeskins, as well as man-made objects such as bits of glass, paper and metal foil. Furthermore, males paint their bowers, using a mixture of charcoal and saliva to produce a black 'paint'; this is applied with a piece of fibrous bark, used more like a sponge-applicator than a brush, held in the beak. Displays by the male are very vocal and include dancing with tail held aloft and leaping over the bower.

Remarks: This is a common species and is perhaps the best-known and most fully studied of all the bowerbirds. It feeds on fruits and berries, and some insects, and is gregarious outside the breeding season, forming flocks of up to a hundred birds.

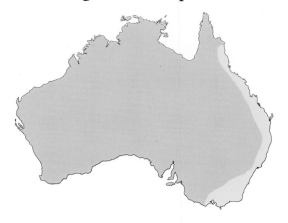

Great or Great Grey Bowerbird

Chlamydera nuchalis

Great or Great Grey Bowerbird

Chlamydera nuchalis

Distribution: Australia, in the extreme north from northern-most Western Australia across to the Cairns area of northern Queensland.

Description: 340–380 mm (*13½–15 in*). The sexes are more or less alike. The whole head is ash-grey, with a bright pink or lilac crest at the nape, and the upperparts are pale greyish-brown with pale tips to the feathers, the underparts almost wholly greyish-buff.

Breeding: Polygamous. A bulky but loosely-made shallow nest of sticks and twigs lined with leaves is built in fairly open vegetation up to 9 m (*30 ft*) above the ground, and one or two eggs are laid, pale greenish or creamy marked with a maze of brown and black spots and hairstreaks. Bowers are made in groups and each male maintains his own. These are not unlike those of the Spotted Bowerbird in general construction, layout and dimensions, but the walls may join above the platform to form a loose tunnel. Decorative material includes large numbers of stones, wallaby bones, shells (land-shells and, at the coast, seashells – and also coral), leaves, fruits, seeds and other vegetable matter, bits of green cloth, glass or metal – and so forth. These are laid at the ends of the avenue or platform. Apparent bower painting has been observed, but this remains to be confirmed.

Remarks: This is a fairly common species in the wetter areas of northernmost Australia and one which frequently lives close to human habitation, even building bowers around, on and occasionally inside houses. It has a colourful reputation as a thief, stealing all manner of small articles from man to use in bower decoration. It is the largest of the bowerbirds.

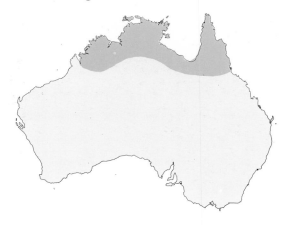

Lauterbach's Bowerbird

Chlamydera lauterbachi

Lauterbach's Bowerbird

Chlamydera lauterbachi

Distribution: New Guinea, in parts of the low and mid-mountain grasslands of the main body of the island, from sea level to 1800 m (*5800 ft*).

Description: 265 mm (*10½ in*). The sexes are alike. The crown is yellowish-olive and the upperparts are generally olive-brown, with yellowish or buffish edges to the feathers; the tail has a yellowish-white tip. The throat is yellowish, streaked with brown, and the remaining underparts are pale yellow, with broad brown streaks on the upper breast and some barring on the flanks.

Breeding: Polygamous. The nest is a flimsy, open cup of stems, vines and grasses built in a sapling or in cane-grass. One pale greenish egg is laid, scrawled with brown streaks and hairlines. The bower of this species is unique in having four walls: the basic *Chlamydera*-type platform or avenue of interwoven sticks is built, with side walls of sticks up to 60 cm (*2 ft*) high and angled outwards rather than vertical, but also with longer cross-walls of similar construction at either end, forming an enclosed chamber in which a bird is virtually hidden from view. Stones are the main ornaments used, but blue berries also occur. An important recent discovery, first described in 1966, is that this is another bower painter: the material used has not been identified, but it is mixed with saliva during mastication in the bill and produces a whitish 'paint'.

Remarks: This species is locally common in old grass and canefield areas with scattered bushes and trees. The food is mainly fruits, but also includes some insects. The bird was discovered by the German botanist C. Lauterbach and named after him.

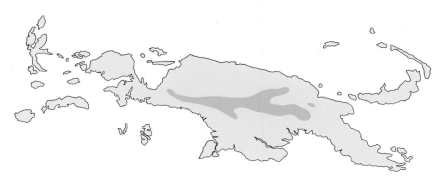

Spotted Bowerbird

Chlamydera maculata (above)

Fawn-breasted Bowerbird

Chlamydera cerviniventris (below)

Spotted Bowerbird

Chlamydera maculata

Distribution: Australia, one population in the east from central Queensland south to New South Wales and Victoria, the other west from South into Western Australia.

Description: 270–280 mm (*11–11½ in*). The sexes are alike: the crown and face are mottled dark brown and blackish-brown, with an erectile tuft of iridescent violet-pink on the nape – often smaller in females. The hind neck is grey-brown and the remaining upperparts are blackish-brown with bold buffish-pink spots. The throat is pinkish, mottled with dark brown, and the rest of the underparts are pale buff, barred grey-brown on the flanks. Western birds are paler, more indistinctly spotted than eastern.

Breeding: Polygamous. A fragile, shallow nest is made of small sticks and twigs and lined with a few leaves, placed at varying heights in saplings and trees, and in this two (rarely three) eggs are laid, pale greenish-yellow with dark scrawls, lines and hairstreaks. Males build bowers in groups, each maintaining his own. The bower is usually near water and is a mat-like structure of interwoven sticks, up to about 2 m (*6 or 7 ft*) long, with walls of sticks 25 to 50 cm (*10 to 20 in*) high, and is extensively decorated with large amounts of ornamental material, especially bleached rabbit and sheep bones, and white or grey pebbles and snail shells, but also including berries, pine cones and bits of glass. This bird is another 'bower painter': males produce a reddish-brown paint of saliva and grass, masticated in the beak and smeared onto the bower walls.

Remarks: A rather scarce and elusive bird, it is reputed to be a mimic. It is a bird of semi-open country with scattered trees and scrub, feeding mainly on fruits and berries, and some insects.

Fawn-breasted Bowerbird

Chlamydera cerviniventris

Distribution: Australia – Cape York and thence across the Torres Straits islands to New Guinea, where it is found around the perimeter of the eastern half of the main island and in one area on the Vogelkop.

Description: 270–280 mm (*11–11½ in*). The sexes are alike. Apart from some grey on the crown and some grey-brown streaking on the face and throat, the bird is more or less uniform brown above, lightly spotted with buffish-white; the underparts are cinnamon-buff with some dark streaking on the breast.

Breeding: Presumably polygamous. The nest is a loose cup of small sticks, built at no great height in a tree, in which one or two eggs are laid, creamy coloured with dark lines and scratches. The bower is not unlike those of the other *Chlamydera* species, with an avenue of interwoven sticks and two side-walls of sticks, but with a spreading platform at either end – one being rather larger than the other. Decorative items are usually placed on the larger platform and are apparently almost always green – fruits and fresh leaves. The displays connected with these bowers, and the organization of the males using them, have been incompletely described.

Remarks: This species occurs in savannah with scattered trees and bushes, often close to beaches and swamps and never far from the coast. It is fairly common in Cape York and in the southern part of its range in New Guinea, but much less so in northern New Guinea. The main food is fruits and berries, but some insects are also taken.

Index

BIBLIOGRAPHY
Gilliard, E. T.: *Birds of Paradise and Bowerbirds*, London, Weidenfeld & Nicolson, 1969.
Rand, A. L. & Gilliard, E. T.: *Handbook of New Guinea Birds*, London, Weidenfeld & Nicolson, 1967.
Mackay, R. D.: *The Birds of Port Moresby and District*, Melbourne, Thomas Nelson, 1970.
Iredale, T.: *Birds of Paradise and Bowerbirds*, Melbourne, Georgian House, 1950.
Macdonald, J. D.: *Birds of Australia*, Sydney, A. H. & A. E. Reed, 1973.